Baby Dara and the Sahara

Barry Loftus

Interior Formatting and cover design by Dorothy Dreyer
Editor: Niall MacGiolla Bhuí
Reviewer: Karen Gallen
Cover photography by Aaron Hennessy

Published by Book Hub Publishing, An Independent Publishing House, Galway and Limerick, Ireland. www.bookhubpublishing.com

ISBN: 978-1-7396189-2-6

*Book Hub Publishing uses paper sourced only from sustainable forestry. We are committed to diversity, inclusion and equality.

For Ross Maitiú

Heff, we miss you.

Acknowledgements

I would like to thank my wife Alma, you are my Yin and know me better than anyone. My three kids - the lights of my life, Danny, Naoise and baby Dara. My Mam, Dad and brother Niall for all their love and support. Mam, I Understand now why you hoped I had ten kids just like me.

My lads, especially Neil, Martin, John and the original editor Rory, my coaches Stephen Donnelly, Darren Siggins and Mairead Gordon.

I want to thank my customers at Strand Fitness, James Geraghty, Mark, Finn O'Meara, and my Tent 80 mates Aaron, Seamus, Jack, Ian, Alan, Jonathan and Ronan for their support and leadership.

Laura, I will never forget all you did whilst Alma was in hospital.

All the midwives and staff of SCBU in Castlebar, St. Monica's maternity ward, NICU and the Coombe, Grainne & Colm and Baby Ross Maitiú 3.12.20, James Carty, Mark and Yvonne, Mossy, Hugh's House for their amazing space, everyone that supported me, Strand Fitness and donated towards the fund for Hugh's House, Mary Corcoran and all the crew in Mullimore who helped with the kids when we were up the walls.

The community of Crossmolina and beyond that lit candles and continue to do so for others saying nothing, but just actioning things with the very best hearts. A village raises a child.

My publisher, Susan from Book Hub Publishing and writing mentor, Niall from ShadowScript Ghostwriters who took a chance on me and this book. They have helped me become a better writer in a brief space of time.

Endorsements

"This has undoubtedly been the most demanding physical and mental challenge I've ever embraced. The MDS, a 250km rollercoaster ride that takes you from the highest peaks of elation to the darkest corners of your mind in an instant. Throughout this journey, I found myself questioning my abilities and purpose. Thankfully, despite the often unattractive struggle, I managed to fend off the inner doubts and cross the finish line. While the path was frequently arduous, the sense of camaraderie we built in Tent 80 provided an incredible support system. The encouragement, determination, honest guidance and constructive criticism that was freely given humbled me. In those moments, I realised I was never alone...

I want to express my gratitude to Barry, the first member of Tent 80 I met. Barry had an uncanny knack for providing just the right push at the opportune moment, offering a reassuring smile when needed, or delivering those motivating words to keep me going. Thank you, Barry, for your unwavering support and timely encouragement. And I should add, of course...Up the DEISE."

—Aaron Hennessy

"MDS 2023 was everything it was supposed to be - a savagely tough course; endless sand dunes; steep Jebel climbs; technical rocky descents; wadi crossings; rough open ground; searing temperatures hitting 52 C; sleeping each night in basic, communal Berber tents with frequent sandstorms ripping through the camp, knocking down tents and scattering gear everywhere. Self-supported, carrying all your own food and kit for the week on your back, it was a genuine test of physical and mental endurance."

—Ian McClelland

"Slow is smooth and smooth is fast!"

—Jack Norris

"Every single day was individually the hardest thing I have ever done. It was brutal and has shifted my entire perspective on life. Nobody should do this race - I cannot wait to go back."

—Ronan Kirby

"For me, the MDS was both a very selfish and very generous experience. Selfish because it took hours of training and preparation to get my body and mind into a state where I could credibly attempt an adventure which has been completed by fewer people than have climbed Mount Everest [I'll check the validity of this]. Selfish because it cost so much. Selfish because it's all consuming. Generous because in the MDS, as a participant, we give all our spare time and holiday allocation to achieve something which hopefully makes us individually a better person. It takes me out of the normal hum-drum status-quo of daily life. They designed the MDS to get you right back to the fundamental principles of surviving and co-existing with fellow humans. No phones, no opting out, no guarantees of finishing, no change of plans. Just like life, there's just no safety net for what's thrown at you and how you cope.
On the long day, as I headed into the final 40km in darkness with a whole heap of pain, I had to take a step back. I was

close to the edge. The edge of what, I'm not sure. I took a reset physically and mentally. In my mind, I invited those I'd held dear to revisit. I experienced a myriad of emotional waves, both enriching and quite unexpected. The desert is a place to be experienced. The desert gives you spiritual time-out.

My mates in tent number 80 of MDS 2023 are truly exceptional. Through sandstorms, snoring and sharing limited rations, we managed exceptionally well. Respect for each other was our glue.

So for me, the MDS was both a very selfish and very generous experience. I really hope the overall net result makes me a more generous person to those around me.

People ask me if I believe they could complete the MDS. It's not actually about the race, it's about your approach to life and the challenges it brings. It's about making decisions and sticking with the outcomes. Attitude determines success or failure. Henry Ford articulated this very well,

"Whether you think you can, or you think you can't, you're right."

—Seamus Lynch

"MDS is a roller coaster of emotions of self-belief & doubt, failure & success etc. often within the same thought. The best of athletes fall foul of diarrhoea, dehydration, feet blisters, stomach cramps, heat stress etc. the list is endless... It's a very, very tough event that will exhaust every single body system and leave you absolutely drained, both mentally & physically..."

—Alan Heaney

Table of Contents

The Heart in Meditation

The feeling of the heart in a meditation, the feeling of connection of the heart, the body, and mind. The feeling of euphoria when the connection allows for frequencies, allows for emotion, allows for warmth, allows for all these connections to flow within the body. All brought on through a Dr Joe Dispenza meditation. The possibilities of this heart/brain connection of waves are endless. Emotions impact the body's internal mechanisms, systems, and structures like a tide. Just by sitting upright, listening and allowing. Such is the power of this emotion, such is the power of the heart/brain connection. It is truly amazing what we can achieve in this state, but yet not trying to achieve anything other than the connection that the designs of which are trying to create by linking the energies available. Your heart connecting to your mind, like a road from one town to another. While you breathe, deeply in a relaxed Alpha state.

When I had a chance to talk, in my then Citroen Berlingo parked outside Castlebar hospital, when I called my mother and bawled my eyes out, soon after that road that links the heart and brain became blocked. It is, to this day, still blocked. After that, then release of emotion to my mother. I did not have any other emotion for the duration of this pregnancy; I repressed all feeling and lived from my chin up, entering and staying in a high range Beta wave throughout saying things like I'm 100%, or hashtag, get on with it, both in person and online. Therefore, all you will read is from a height, an observation rather than internal because to deal with what was happening in real time as a very emotional man I had to become someone or something else namely a very unemotional man and my writing reflects this. Dara is written in high Beta wave, whereas the Sahara is written in an Alpha wave.

After those first tears, it was years in a desert before I cried again.

What We Have, We Hold

Lying in my son's bed arming myself with information that I could not process, I was dumping my thoughts into a dark web. The uncomfortable realisation was that I felt that the best thing to happen was for this baby to pass to the other side quickly and painlessly. I was uncomfortable; I was worried and thought that there was something wrong with me for having these inclinations.

I had a fright; I was frightened, frightened at what was ahead of us, at what I was going to experience or not experience, frightened at my own thoughts. Imagining now where a fright becomes reality, where those that live in this experience do not wake up from this nightmare but spend days, weeks and months crying themselves to sleep, only to wake up with sodden tears once more. Who am I to write this book when my only experience was to get a fright when there are those that have to make decisions that even today in 2023 are so taboo that we must not talk, we must not say for fear of upsetting the person behind a linen curtain looking outside their homestead. I got a fright but there are those that walk down a maternity hall with their deceased child in a Moses basket or box whilst the ward doors are closed and midwives look away in respect, imagine that long hall and its long walk or wheelchair roll to exit a space of life that gets closed off to stave the upset of doting parents now sporting a cooling device under a Moses basket. How can I worry about my chances of success when there are mothers who already know their child will not survive and must endure the rest of their pregnancy with that knowledge?.

What gets me is the rooms that were shared at different times, in different seasons, to different couples with different outcomes. During autumn, the horse chestnut tree outside our maternity window saw a different result compared to another couple in a similar position when winter arrived..

These couples and single mothers face a layered life with percentages and probabilities, leading to the same end fate. It is alright for you to wish the best outcome that allows some grace, but not all will think that way and that is alright too, for we are not all the same. It's okay to wear a sheet of stainless steel around your head to keep positive thoughts and block out negativity. It's also okay to hope for a speedy recovery, seek support, or prefer to be alone. It's okay to hope for the best result with some leniency, but not everyone shares that view, and that's okay because we're different. There is no handbook, in fact there is so little information to make matters that bit crueller.

We may not colour all the grey areas in our lifetime. There are stigmas that may never go away, but that does not mean that one should be bound by what has happened before as the situation we found ourselves in was unique to us and I dealt with it as best I could. This does not make me a bad person for wanting this life that I had helped create to find a peaceful and painless ending based on what I knew, nor does the person who wants to hold out and explore every avenue feel that their search is foolhardy.

What I kept repeating to myself ad nauseum was "what we have we hold" as in our two babies at the time. Repeating this to myself like a mantra helped me cope, but everyone's process is different. I wouldn't wish this on anyone, as it makes you question life's meaning.

Edwards' syndrome

Edwards' syndrome was first reported by Edwards et al. in 1960, it is also called a trisomy 18 syndrome and because of the extra copy of chromosome 18. There are three variations of Edwards' syndrome - complete, partial, and mosaic trisomy 18.

The most common form of Edwards' syndrome is complete trisomy 18. In this type of syndrome, every cell "contains three complete copies of chromosome 18" (Balasundaram et al., 2022). Mosaic trisomy comes next with 5% of all cases with partial trisomy 18 accounting for 2% of Edwards' syndrome cases (Balasundaram et al., 2022).

The prevalence of Edwards' syndrome ranges from 1 birth in 3,600 to 1 birth in 10,000 cases (Balasundaram et al., 2022). However, over the last number of decades, this is increasing because of an increase in the average maternal age. The prevalence is higher in females compared to males, but females have a better chance of survival than males (Balasundaram et al.,2022).

Edwards' syndrome can be diagnosed prenatally using "antenatal screening with maternal age, maternal serum marker or by the use of ultrasound during the second trimester" (Balasundaram et al., 2022).

There are several neurological, craniofacial, skeletal, cardiovascular, pulmonary, gastrointestinal, genitourinary and central nervous system malformations in these antenatal screens, serum markers and ultrasounds. These are some images that I had google imaged the night they informed me of what was wrong with our baby's scan. It was quite distressing, and I can only imagine the distress of parents that receive diagnosis of these conditions daily around the world. I do not know why I searched for an image. I wanted quick answers, and those quick answers were of images that I was not prepared for. Imagining what it would have been like to see those images upon our own labyrinth screen is not something that I do, but some have to experience this, and this is an incredibly hard cruelty of life for any parent. To be so joyous one moment to being distraught the next, many maybe do not understand how internally breaking this must be. Having been there for Danny and Naoise's scans, expecting parents to see features like noses and already see similarities, be they real or imagined within others of their lineage. Being in that labyrinth waiting for features to come into a screen with our baby curled up in a ball is nothing compared to the distress others have faced in similar positions having to witness a part of themselves on a screen undergoing the complexities of chromosomal imbalances.

For these parents to function thereafter is a testament to their own strength and resilience to find something to hold on to, to drive on with their lives but yet be present.

Doctors cannot provide a definitive treatment for Edwards' syndrome, and they also face ethical issues when developing treatment plans for new-borns (Balasundaram et al., 2022). This is because of the high mortality rate of babies with this condition. Nearly 40% of diagnosed babies die during labor, and one third of these babies are born preterm (Balasundaram et al., 2022).

The median survival for these babies goes from 3 days until 14.5 days, the percentages for survival are 60%-75% in the first week, 20%-40% at one month and 10% at one year (Balasundaram et al., 2022).

It's hard to stay positive when we don't understand how our baby could experience neurological instability, cardiac failure, and respiratory failure (Balasundaram et al., 2022). There are cases of some babies living healthy lives with this syndrome here (Alshami et al., 2020) noted a 26-year-old continuing to live well. This may show the importance of early detection and parental education on the intricacies of dealing with such a difficult situation.

I don't envy anyone in this position, but one or two parents and a support network can do amazing things when faced with adversity and require true resilience.

Armed with all this information, I was really in a terrible place. I could have called so many people with my parents away and my mother, a mid-wife, being away must have been so hard on them as well. I just laid there in my son's bed. Laying there wishing for this bad dream to be all over, wishing myself to sleep away from this bad dream.

I would love to write and explain how I found resilience, how I powered on, how I created a template for others to follow, but with my worst-case scenario thinking, my thoughts were counterproductive and negative. I did not have the hope that was needed in this situation. I thought that what we have is what we hold and I was totally focused on what was now best for Alma.

Without the strength of others, I just kept repeating to myself, "What we have we hold" repeatedly. Without knowledge of what is possible or the knowing what the issue was exactly, unfortunately I just focused on the imagery and wording that comes with google searches as I knew no better.

"What we have we hold" repeatedly like the words would wash some sort of safety catch over the situation we now found ourselves in, hoping words would seep into the cracks showing in my life like a resin building my world back up.

There is no right way or wrong way to react. We all react differently. Looking back, I wish I was more positive as I am not naturally a glass half full type of person. It is easy to lose hope in situations where information is limited or conflicting, and those who read these words may recognise this, I think. One medical professional could ask you to make the process as easy as possible and the closest hospital to home as allowable in order to deal with the ramifications of what a screen may or may not present, or depending on the Syndrome, the next may say "ok, your baby may not play for Liverpool but how about an Olympic gold in the Special Olympics in 20-odd years' time".

Taking a sheet of metal and bending it around your head in order to keep the negativity out and positivity in may be one of the best tools that one can employ here. The Harmony test shows parents if their baby has a high or low risk of Down Syndrome, Edwards' Syndrome, or Patau Syndrome by using cell-free DNA in the mother's blood.

Rather than thinking morbidly and bottling up emotions and worries that you may have done wrong, know that in these instances there is nothing you have done wrong. It is what it is. You may have some tough times or you may embark on a journey that you, your partner and other children, will see as a positive experience where first steps, smiles and laugh out loud moments may well happen.

References

Alshami, A., Douedi, S., Guida, M., Ajam, F., Desai, D., Zales, V. and Calderon, D.M., 2020. Unusual longevity of edwards syndrome: a case report. Genes, 11(12), p.1466

Balasundaram, P. and Avulakunta, I.D., 2022. Edwards Syndrome. In StatPearls [Internet]. StatPearls Publishing.

1. The Labyrinth

I see our baby. It's in a ball. I think it looks like it is in pain.

Life can change in an instant. Sitting together with my wife, Alma, waiting for our baby's 22week scan in Castlebar Hospital, Co. Mayo, I was more concerned about getting the heat on in my hot studio for the evening classes than thinking that this scan might be anything more than much like the rest were a formality. Part of the process. Great to be there, great to see everything and hear about everything going well first hand. But this was not our first rodeo. I'm busy. Life is busy. These waiting rooms are full of many people of various creeds and colours, and I find this fascinating. All looking at each other and wondering. All sitting, waiting. Waiting to see.

Back then it was a given, having an expectant wife and going through the pregnancy process. I never once looked and thought about the person and or couple behind that pregnancy. What they were going through. What they had gone through. Their journey, whether or not as a couple, was their own. It was all a formality to me, thoughts of a youthful man, albeit now middle-aged, a father of two yet inexperienced in all things life and loss.

This waiting area was more like a train station than an actual waiting room. A constant hum of noise and movement. Now, maybe I imagined looks of apprehension. Maybe I was oblivious to what really happens in these places, coming from an attitude of �hunky dory’, �everything is rosy’. I cannot remember the specific faces, but I do imagine what those faces were and the looks upon them. Burrowed frowns maybe? Or perhaps maybe that is my mind’s way of dealing with what was going to happen soon.

They directed us once we were called. Directed away from the staging post with all its random people and uncomfortable chairs. Directed into a tiny room that was cool on the skin. So claustrophobic. Three people were in a tiny room with what seemed like a huge scanning machine alongside a matching bed. The lights dimmed to nothing, illuminated with the glare of the screens. We could well have been in a labyrinth. A labyrinth far underground where a different being lives. A different being or beings that is controlled and directed by this machine. An eye that holds the present and the future, an eye that has all the power. The power of your thoughts and your feelings. This eye has the power to change everything forever. And it knows it, it is punch drunk with power. Laid on by whomever created it.

Maybe a Saxon with their glorious history in creating these all-consuming devices manufactured in some contested land, like the Ruhr valley. Deep within our new labyrinth. Where once happy, chatty and chirpy, we fall down. We lose control and cede power to this eye. Where now we are as much a statistic and a percentage as a couple observing their future deep in this labyrinth. We wait and wait, deeper we fall. An overworked and underpaid sonographer. Doing her best, doing all she can do with this wand. A wand held gently but connected to an eye. It is so cold in this room and as what should be a formality drags. Where in previous similar situations I can remember seeing my son's spine for the first time or my daughter's appendages. Here, now - nothing is forthcoming.

To make us feel better and less worried, an organ is found. However, even with my own lack of experience and knowledge. Even being a man here, I was about as useful as a chocolate teapot. In these situations, where most of the time the best course of action is tobkeep the mouth shut and hold a hand. I can't help but feel the worry wash over me as I fall deeper into this black space, losing control all the while. Tears flow down Alma's cheeks. This is not supposed to happen to us. This sort of thing happens to other people, other couples. Are we going to become another number? I was not prepared for this. Not prepared for bad news. It is not in the script. It was our third pregnancy. Equals third baby.

What's the issue?

Something is wrong.

It does not need to be said really, there is no script. There are no apps. It is a change in

circumstance that happens over seconds. A change in direction of time and energy that was once headed in a specific direction but has now completely flipped upon itself and sealed its fate within that room. This machine is the ruler and executioner. It feels no love or pain; it sees into the deepest recesses of a human unbeknownst to that being, not to a cellular level, but pretty damn close. Close enough for comfort. Something is wrong. Badly wrong.

A senior sonographer is summonsed to the room. Now there are four of us in this tiny room with this eye now frantically moving back and forth searching. Searching, searching for something. Still in control. An all-controlling eye. It has taken over. Information is now becoming scanter and rather than going about our daily business, all smiles and thanks, wishes of luck and details of further scans, we now are on a different course. A course that I do not now control or understand.

I see our baby. It's in a ball. I think it looks like it is in pain.

2. A Bit of a Shock

Without experience, with no knowledge, with no schooling, there is a mode or switch that Dads seem to possess. They do not reveal it in MRI's, X-rays, CT's or autopsies. But it is there. It was made a part of the wiring, I believe. Maybe about the time when a newborn would look like the father initially in order for bonding, safety and protection. It lays dormant maybe for years, maybe forever, unless enacted. I can remember exactly where I was in the hallway outside the dark labyrinth when this circuit board was powered up and this mode was turned on.

Once powered up this circuit board much like a motherboard fires up all the love, concern and emotion that a man may or may not have known existed. Here, the toughest of the tough have melted. Melted away all of their scars and hardened knuckles, unable even to punch a wall now. One of the greatest pieces of male biology manifests itself outwardly as pacing the hallways with a lost look upon a furrowed face. Many of us have been there.

With Alma now being moved from the labyrinth and being taken upstairs to another windowless posting, worlds fall away only to be matched with time, which seems to have lost any meaning. I cancel my evening's classes abruptly as more important issues take hold. Things that were once important now fade away. Fade away to nothing. All that was built is unimportant now. Everything seems to lie in the fate of these walls which are closing in on me. I find it hard to breathe. The only tools I have to offer are of comfort and comforting.

An experienced midwife enters the fray. "Ye have had a bit of a shock".

Yes. Yes, we have. Do we look shocked, I wonder? Am I now in shock? Or is this just what midwives say in these situations? I am beginning to take apart words and sentences and analyse everything being said and cross-referencing body language. Trying to eke out as much information as possible without actually asking anything. Especially in front of Alma. I just stand there drilling my eyes into skulls. Nearly scanning waves of language as words leave orifices and into the ether of this now prison cell like room where everything seems to be ready for war gaming if anything were to kick off. As Alma is now being admitted into the ward of this maternity wing some 20 weeks too early, I leave to tie up loose ends, moving up and down hospital stairs with no patience for lifts.

I meet a medical professional involved in the now unfolding nightmare we find ourselves in. These roles are not envious positions, especially in the current world in which we live, one of litigation and general abuse towards these professions. Everyone with half a brain knows the pressure that the staff experience on a day-to-day basis and is still under here, especially in Castlebar. I am empathetic as my mother was a nurse and midwife, but I want and need to know exactly what is going on.

Towering over her, I try not to be physically impeding, overshadowing her own sense of wellbeing. But yet I feel my shoulders spreading as a defence mechanism. I eyeball without wanting to be aggressive, but am overly concerned. I corner her. I put her on the spot and I ask her what did she see or not see? What is wrong?

She said to me. “I think your baby has Edwards’ Syndrome.”

3. The Corner Room

I thanked her for being straight with me. Internally, I was wondering what the feck Edwards' Syndrome was only weighing the syndrome wording and knowing that it could not be too good. These words held me down, as they were stored somewhere within my conscious and subconscious. Words that were not to be uttered as I returned to Alma who was now admitted to hospital.

There was no time for researching anything, even though time had slowed down to a trickle. In her maternity room, being cared for by a team of midwives, I was encouraged to jump in the hospital bed and snuggle my wife like a prescription as if this had been

Studied. The benefits of being held for a long period, in this time, seemed the best option. An older source of protection, arms around two within one. There is a horse chestnut tree outside the room in between the hospital and the old building across the road. I wondered what that tree has seen in the window of this maternity room and ward over the years. How many happy and sad moments has it seen through the seasons? This season now being late summer with a heavy green tree hulking over the window. As we lay together somewhat stunned but with natural fight responses possibly fired up within ourselves, we watched a documentary about the Kerry football legend, Mick O' Dwyer.

The sound of his voice was so comforting, watching how his life unfolded in black and white, his success on and off the pitch lit up the room somewhat. Images then of Waterville where I surfed a secret spot on a Takayama model T many years ago–a beautiful lefthand point break guarded by a gatekeeper rock. This heavy board shaped for the point breaks of Malibu stuck in the pocket as I went rail to rail. Waves I can still remember to this day. The image of this point break rests on our sitting room wall, a wedding present from a warm Cork man. Everything is connected, it seems by water or voice. His voice, his life the way of life had a short-term analgesic effect which was complemented with the now full noble tree outside. Two pillars propping me up and helping me stand process with the information that was now bounding off the insides of my unknowledgeable brain, whilst I tried to wrap my arms around Alma and make this situation we now found ourselves in, just go away trying to squeeze it away. I was in a state of limbo, only broken by the regular midwife checks on Alma.

4. Falling Apart

When I left Alma at the hospital to sort out something as trivial as moving one of our two cars from the car park, it was then that I first started relying on my friends and family. Traversing the Castlebar to Crossmolina road via Pontoon in County Mayo is bad enough as an over and back, never mind the now third trip with my buddy, Murphy and his then fiancée, Reynagh. Being a few steps ahead in marital time, I am sure it opened a window into some of the stressors and stresses. Trying to converse as normally as possible but incoherent and worrisome, no doubt.

Myself and Alma are just a few steps ahead having started a family with two healthy babies already, and this episode shone a light on what may or may not be ahead of them.

Being on that road so many times with its boggy lumps and bumps, long winding turns into sharp decelerations. No matter how many times it gets resurfaced, it always ends up feeling the same. The same roll under the tyres coupled with the same hazards. This road is a constant that time is so slow to change. A 1980s style road that will remind you of simplicity and misery of featureless cars that could go as quick but were slower with less comfort. Sliding from one side to another, drawing smiley faces on fogged up windows.

How I would like to be transported back to those simpler times when daydreams did not contain any real-world scenarios. Being late summer with trees full and colourful bogs emptied of turf. Sometimes scarred rocks and walls which fended off previous fires but now are covered in lichen, watching every move since time began. There is nothing that can be done with this road. Its only actual change will be flying cars, which will add a different dimension of the same look. It is a cross the locality and localities will bear. For whatever reasons, good or bad, season to season, year to year, it will never change, bringing more happy and sad times, each of these journeys leaving cookies. Some revisited when a bump brings two or more neurons together to reminisce.

With one car less in the car park, I made my way back to the room flanked by that great horse chestnut tree. Going up to say goodnight and goodbye. The most unnatural moments, going only to leave again. I was present when the Doppler came out. I had the presence of mind to record it this time. I can still see and hear those initial heart beats to this day some five years later. Racing at what seemed to be a hundred miles an hour. The baby that I had seen curled up in an uncomfortable ball, maybe scared–what I thought at the time was in pain with a heart of a lion. I was so proud to hear that heartbeat beating so fast and so strong.

I left it all behind to make my way home, stopping briefly to call my own parents with the news. For the first and last moment, I broke down. As a late thirty-year-old man, I was only thirteen talking to Mammy and Daddy about our child and what was to be their fourth grandchild. Losing all control after hours of build-up of emotion and worry. Loss of control and statistics. Having our lives turned upside down for what should have been a formality, after the scan, we were now on a road that so many have also sadly travelled. I travelled back home to Crossmolina once more. Back to an empty quiet house as our three-year-old boy Danny and two-year-old daughter Naoise were staying with their maternal grandparents. Back to an empty house that is and was always so noisy. The only peace in the house is when curtains are closed and stories read. Previously yearning for quiet time, I was now begging for my two babies to be there, jumping on top of me and the sound of Paw Patrol coming from the television. Anything but quiet.

A few weeks earlier I had taken my last alcoholic drink, having listened to "How to control your drinking" by Alan Carr on Audible. I was an IPA and red wine fan. Thinking back then I had a problem, my last drink as recommended in the book, was something you would not normally drink. Turned out to be a Jameson whiskey neat. This last alcoholic drink– taken the same summer a few weeks prior to post completion of my seventh Ironman Triathlon. I quit drinking. A bit backwards, but a step forward for me. Lying now in my son's bed as I could not settle in my own, I could only comfort myself with his scent on his duvet rather than the velvet of a red wine. Even though it was still bright, in an unnaturally empty house in my three-year-old boy's bunkbed, I slept. Without the aid of alcohol, I do not think I ever felt as lonely and vulnerable. Still, thankfully, the next morning I was not adding to everything with the grogginess of a bottle of red wine. Around 6 am I rose and headed for the Ballina AC run track. I thought it best to practice what I preached, in good times and in bad, to get out there and get some training in as I was on a programme for the Dublin City Marathon that year. I cannot remember what was exactly on my programme that morning. I decided a speed session upon. The run track is a natural amphitheatre. In the early morning light, with nobody else around, it can be quite peaceful bar the drum of traffic on the town's approaching roads. With the light washing over the dewy grassy hills overlooking the track, I did my warmup. Speed sessions are love/hate. There is always that gross feeling prior to doing one, but once the engine is revved up, one just gets it done. The post session feel is probably the best of any session you may do of a week. Such is the release of endorphins and chemicals around the body after a hard session willing oneself around a four hundred metre tartan track trying to stick to the numbers as prescribed by my coach, Stephen, on my watch. Normally, I go off too fast in the first effort going to about 3:30 per min km pace. My body's engine management lights come on and then slow down to closer to sub 4 min pace. I generally struggle with the middle efforts, but always finishing strong or on point.

That morning, however, my legs were like jelly. After I warmed up–I could hardly move, never mind go flat to the mat. Physically, my body was either telling me to stop or the build-up of stress and emotion was tripping some sort of switch that was saying no.

After the effort of getting in, the strong man, the David Gogginsesqe attitude to life. He, the man who wrote "Can't Hurt Me", the story of an overweight man who changed his life to become a United States Navy Seal and accomplished Ultra Runner. I just peeled myself off that track hardly able to get back to my car which was parked on site. I would not say I was in a mess. But certainly I could not function as normal.

5. Melman

I returned to the maternity ward later that morning on what was to be day two but, more importantly, twenty-two weeks' gestation plus 1. There is a security door to gain entry into the ward more to ward off over exuberant friends and families than prevent anything sinister. It stops the flow and when it opens, it reveals a different world. Expectant mothers walking around in dressing gowns with their hands on their lumbar spine and or tummy. Uncomfortable. The odd expectant or fully fledged Dad, unshaven and bedraggled. Where a greeting here is a wink, and or a head movement. Not a code per se, but enough for the flow.

One hears about pillars of society at funerals or in court. The difference he or she made. What they did and all that they brought with them. What they created or spent, what they bought and the legacy left behind them. Upon a flurry of junior doctors scurrying about the consultant at arms, I encountered two pillars that morning. One offering and delivering with permission a hug. But not any ordinary hug. A nurse hug, a mammy hug, a hug that reminded me of being picked up as a boy whilst in for a grommet operation one night in Sligo General. A hug that spanned time and allowed my head to rest on what seemed like boulders. It was a hug that was needed, in the middle of a ward, in the middle of a hospital, in the middle of Castlebar. Time stood still as I glanced a smile from administrative staff that were also well versed in all the goings on of these well-worn halls. For all the hugs and care, our immediate future now seemed to fall into the huge physical hands of the consultant. Telling us a story of a child and mother he meets that he thought at the time, based on his knowledge, would not make it. He tells us about meeting this now person as he laughs and enjoys every bit about being wrong.

No decisions are made yet, but with the junior doctors talking among themselves having been privy to conversations, I get the inside information that we are being transferred to Dublin for second opinions but indications are not positive, for all the will in the world. Trying to stay as positive as possible for Alma, but yet knowing all I knew at that point releasing none of that information to her. I wanted to know what all the other eventualities were based on what was in front of me.

I am not a control freak, but I like to stay informed. So, in the eventuality of the worst possible outcome, or outcomes at least, I could be a bit more supportive through being prepared rather than being a mess. I called my uncle Enda, a funeral director. I asked him what happens here regarding the baby if it does not make it which, all indications were now pointing to.

"There is no protocol", he said. "You do not need to worry". The baby can be buried in a grave at home. "The staff in the hospital make up a special box and you can bring it home with you". There were staff members that took care of this within the hospital. Tasked with creating a vessel to carry our baby back down that windy, bumpy road should the need arise.

They do a great job apparently. A grim job, but how important, nonetheless. A job that is being done all the while normal people pass by and through that hospital unbeknownst that there are people that carry out these roles. A job, that is outside the roles of which they are being renumerated and rewarded for. Something that is essential but yet one would not know unless you or someone you know was in these hours of human stress that spans time itself. With this in mind, I could see and get my head around the end of this. If it were to end like this. Calling a mother of a woman I knew from home who had gone through something similar at a similar time, I could build a scaffold of knowledge about what may happen and to somehow be prepared for that. She was very to the point. No BS, just facts. And this is what I wanted. Walking up and down, over and back alongside the old Harlequin Hotel, trying to build a picture of what might happen over the next day or days.

One of my good mates describes me as akin to the giraffe from the movie Madagascar called Melman. If the plane hit turbulence, the plane was going down and we are all going to die. I'm not as bad as that, but every time I chat to him about an injury or whatnot I can catastrophise. What's the worst-case scenario here, and then let's work our way back? The worst-case scenario was a tadpole being born and put in a small white box to be brought home to Crossmolina graveyard on the Erris Road, maybe with a few friends and family around. There were more questions than answers, where the baby would go exactly.

So I rang our local priest.

Yet again, any worries about protocols or whatnot subsided. I was worried about Alma. I was worried about what would happen to her. I was worried that she may have a breakdown and would long for this baby until the end of her days. Worried that this baby was in pain. Still maybe curled up in that ball that I saw the day before. I just wanted the situation to be over so the healing could begin. I just wanted everything to be ok. Even this morning whilst checking Twitter, I came upon a post for baby Andrew who would have been 21 today. ‘Lost at 22 weeks and 3 days. And at the time not allowed to be registered or claim maternity benefit as he was under 24 weeks' (@biker42 twitter)

6. Let Go

It was agreed by all parties that what was the best approach was more opinions. To placate and leave no stone unturned. It was hard to be internally positive when all indications were leading to a wall. Not being allowed to travel with Alma in the ambulance for insurance reasons supposedly, I had to make my own way. Another dog of a road and dog of a drive at the best of times never mind with all the information that was bouncing around my head.

These thoughts are morbid and realistic. Knowing then that this baby was either not going to make it or if it was born soon, it would not live long. All I wanted was for Alma to be ok. If this baby was going to pass, I wanted to minimise the stress that Alma would endure in the present moment. Knowing however, that this sense loss would at the same time stay forever if it happened.

Knowing what I knew then, I was asking for this baby to pass over. Not be in what I perceived as pain, stress or suffering anymore. I continued to wish this child that I had helped bring this far, to let go. Letting go for what was best for him or her and his or her mother. These thoughts were distressing. They were thoughts I would never have dreamed of. Yet they were what I thought were best. On a continuous loop throughout that trip up the road to Holles St in South Dublin City. Wishing this little one to let go. I am surely not the first to think that way, but I wondered, was it gender based or was I a bad person? Wanting the best possible outcome in this position to lead to the least amount of stress for mother and baby. If there was no hope, was it not best for this little one just to pass on? I had heard the Doppler; I had heard the life and the power of that grape-sized heart, but this did not compute with everything else.

Alma, being Alma, chatted the entire way with the accompanying midwife and ambulance driver only to call me to see where I was at various points. Staying positive and uplifted with her whilst I was planning the worst in my head. Morbid to positive, it was a strange experience arriving at Holles St on what was a beautiful late summer morning in the city.

All I had known about Holles St was what I had seen or read about its first female master, Rhona Mahony, as the hospital had been on the national news for various reasons over the years. The building itself has a storied history because of its location and its place in the state's history over the years with all things maternal. Arriving earlier than the ambulance and being able to greet it and enter with Alma, I was really on edge. The building is old, but spattered with new, which is strange going from Edwardian era toilets to brand spanking new waiting areas and rooms. That old internal hospital stone appearance which looks ancient now yet has 1980s vibes which were filled once more with expecting parents, but this time the excitement was replaced with worry and furrowed brows, forced smiles and puffy eyes. Alma was more excited than nervous, hoping for better news with greater scanning equipment here in this hospital.

I had built myself up at this stage to handle all that was going to be said in that room. I researched possible scenarios. I was ready to mind Alma. Even though I knew I could do feck all really, and what I have seen since with other parents of loss, meant a feeling of inadequacy of trying to stop a rising tide with a lid. Couple by couple, they filtered in until it was our turn where we were greeted by a youthful looking yet premiership level of paediatric consultants, a very senior sonographer and a Dutch Junior Doctor who looked so young, fresh and ready to learn, albeit he could be making his confirmation. All those morbid thoughts, unnatural thoughts, all the plans and battle readiness primed to go. I can only imagine how tapped I looked in the corner of this very modern room trying to keep my mouth shut.

7. Confirmation

I can still see this very senior, experienced, and brilliant sonographer clearly turn and block me out as she completely gave all her focus to Alma as she scanned whilst delivering better news. Alma was in tears. I can't remember what I said, or how I said it, but I am sure everything from what I said up to and including my own body language translated to "What the actual fuck are you on about?"

There have been many times in my life that I have been a massive dickhead, and many times of being so unaware, but right there, back then, as that lady ignored me, I could not understand how forty-eight hours previously, I was told that our baby possibly had Edwards' Syndrome. And now this was not the case. It was not what I was saying or not saying, perhaps my body language said it all. It wasn't like I asked her to turn the machine on and off to make sure with a hard reset. Maybe she is just so experienced. She decided it was best to block out the resident dickhead in the room. All these thoughts were internal, but thoughts nonetheless, as I was so overwhelmingly confused with a complete flip of wonderful new information that made absolutely zero sense. At one of these junctures of awareness that now is not the time to speak up. Aware that years of experience has imprinted a stepped process on how to deal with a couple and now male partner in the relationship sitting in the corner, like a corner forward chomping at the bit waiting for the manager and selectors to get the finger out, fill out the slip and send me on to score or burst someone open and into a solid but grassy pitch.

Everything was now where it was supposed to be. Kidneys, arms, legs, head was fine albeit in a different percentile. As she made her way over the heart, which was a quarter the size of a grape, we could see a tiny sliver of tissue growing from one chamber to the next. And told that ‘it will all be grand'. Even the young Dutch buck that made his confirmation the day before piped up with something daft which took the pressure of this corner forward. All these medical professionals combined with these uber sensitive pieces of equipment said to me that there was no more a tadpole in there than there was in me. Alma had what was called a preterm pre-labour rupture of membranes (PPROM). And the biggest negative was that this baby was going to be born in Dublin. On paper a Dub, but only on paper, thank God. This child would be Mayo to the core.

They were so wonderfully easy going and positive. So warm and uplifting. The sea change made a tremendous impact on Alma. Waves and waves of positivity washing over her. I am glad she did not know of the ins and outs, especially those that were plain, incorrect. At this point, with all that was going on and the fact that even though the news was a lot better and we had something to cling onto. We did not know if it was a boy or a girl. With one boy in the house already and one girl, I think I would have liked another boy. Just for a less head melting life. Two lads and a Daddy's princess would be great.

However, and which was actually better - we found out this was not to be the case.

We were having another girl. A girl that they explained, will be helped hopefully to get to 28 weeks' gestation and every other day a bonus after that. Every day inside that womb now counting. Every day, another feature added to a body. Everyday growth. But we were ready to have her as is with whatever she would bring. Even though only hours previously I was wishing for this little one to pass over and not be in stress with her mam anymore, I was now wishing the days of growth but ready to take whatever day she came and do my very best. As long as she could go for a run with her Dad, I was happy. Upon exiting this brilliant white room, all I wanted was some fresh air. Even though the news was great, the walls were all closing in on me. I just wanted to hit the road back down west again. However, I was encouraged/made go for food in the hospital restaurant with Alma and the staff that accompanied us. The restaurant overlooked some of the south city which was really cool. All that life, all that history.

8. Sticky Beans

Some five years on, I can still remember all the faces and comments, chats and brows. Yet, no names. I can see the experience and inexperience. All the learnings and the road to learning. I remember clearly the most uplifting piece of advice from another pillar of a midwife the next day. Another bright summer's morning. Now back in Castlebar.

"The books and consultants say one thing, but it is this baby that will decide what happens".

For all the flurry and flow, it all ground down to who or what this baby is or was going to be. As she was a girl, this then became another positive string in the bow. Girls apparently have a better chance. Maybe evolution or what not. Back in Castlebar, the junior doctors and consultant prepped for possible delivery at 22 weeks plus 3. Going through checks of equipment and paraphernalia, making sure all was there if this baby girl was to come over the next few hours, days, or weeks. Much like putting away the shopping, they seemed to be taking out, checking and putting away reams of small items covered in plastic whilst trying not to make any eye contact.

There were some very hard questions asked at this point. There was no doubt what we wanted. The books and consultants say one thing. This girl another. We are however, very naïve. Inexperienced and just full of hope and wishful thinking. This was only to be a temporary home, though. As with the size of this tot, Alma was to be transferred back to Dublin. We had hoped Holles St. as we felt relationships were built between ourselves and the various consultants, however this was not to be. Alma was to be transferred on her own to the Coombe. I now tried to juggle two kids, a small business and everything in between, with the help of my mam and many others in our community.

Life goes on, these things happen every day and personal economies can't simply grind to a halt. Bills still have to be paid, job roles fulfilled and business ran. Even though Alma was away from her kids and me with super long days. It is all a blur. A blur where a way was lit by the sheer number of candles in the church from genuine folk from all walks of life. I would jibe Alma about her breast-feeding groups, and online groups. With two kids, she seemed to be part of more groups than your average politician.

Groups nearly for each breast that had their own WhatsApp groups and meeting points. There was a battalion of new names and old names, this wan and that wan. She is married to him, ya know yer man you used to play football with. This woman of mine who had moved to these communities pretty recently, had a greater handle of the townlands and people located in these townlands in my opinion for the whole Moy Valley region. I seemed to spend my time saying. Who?

These new mums were and are everywhere. They control the societal fabric and footpaths armed with pocket filled treats, strollers full to the gills for every given scenario from puke to creams with each of them fuelled with immense amounts of caffeine and a newfound hatred of their partner's latest hobby. "He is such a fecking dick" being a favoured comment.

Upon hearing about Alma's situation, one of the girls from Alma's sticky beans (online group based on child's due date) (I shit you not) group rallied the troops and gathered everything from magazines to pocket money for the hospital for her stay in the Coombe. Delivered by courier, from someone I have never met or seen again, it had everything that may be needed. This woman in her own time whilst also pregnant herself had taken the time out to do this for a stranger. Because she felt bad for Alma. What a legend.

And here lies the rub, here it was the fragility of it all when I heard soon after this lady who was so kind lost her own baby. Much like the initial stages of battle where the first gunshots ring out, a woman of such thoughtfulness and kindness ended up being the first one hit. It was so unfair. It took the breath out of me. How tables turned and kept turning for no apparent reasoning.

9 The Ice Man

With Alma's subsequent transfer back up to Dublin and the Coombe, myself and our two other kids remained at home. Three and two years of age, we began a new day-to-day existence. Looking past anything over 24 hours would warp your brain. Thankfully, I had the help of my mother, family, friends, and the local community with my superstar customers at Strand Fitness. After cancelling a full week of classes, I could slot into some sort of groove. Solo, but with a lot of help. Life moves on, albeit slowly and repetitively. Stress would bubble but not spill over, most of the time. It felt like a teetering.

Something small could tip one over the edge. That small thing like the gear box on Alma's VW Tiguan that began to break down. I hope whoever designed that gear box stubs their toes on a weekly basis. Trying to make life work with all the engine management lights beaming doing hard resets in order to get from A to B and make C and D work. Monday to Friday zoomed by and then each weekend - I would travel up to visit Alma and teeny bump in the Coombe, with or without the kids. The first thing we would do is head to the Forty Foot in Dun Laoghaire.

I had done a workshop with Wim Hof, the Iceman, the previous year in Edinburgh, having been given a heads up about him in 2017 by a friend in the military. It was a very surreal experience doing a breathing exercise with Wim and lots of other people. In a large room we listened to Wim belt out Pink Floyd on his guitar whilst we all partook in a breathing exercise oxygenating ourselves as deep as possible to then holding our breath and beginning doing push ups until your body and or lungs could not do anymore. This was the inner fire that was worked upon through physical exercise and the culmination of the day.

Taking a dip in a blow-up pool filled with water and ice of an autumnal sunny day in Edinburgh. Getting into this pool with a load of strangers, experiencing the cold and then beginning to sing together was mad but amazing. The physical and mental change within myself almost instant. From survival to enjoying the experience. This all designed to help him, Wim, deal with the loss of his wife through suicide and bringing up two sons in his own early parental life. The cold unleashing an inner fire to help deal with depression and anxiety. Of all the workshops I have done over the years, from "Little Miss Sunshine" bullshit types to physically or mentally demanding ones, this experience in Edinburgh in a children's blow-up pool stood me well. As when cortisol bubbled about my own system I was drawn to that deep water spot in South Dublin. I would yearn for the moment of getting in all week whilst trying to deal with such banal things as getting lunches ready, getting ready on that slab of eastern rock, walking the steps down holding a rusty rail.

Feeling the initial freeze of autumnal sea water upon my skin–diving in and then moving my body as fast as possible to get warm again and then completely loving the warm wash of adrenaline and chemicals that flowed on and about my body. I honestly believe this reset each weekend helped me throughout this period. I do not think I would have made it without having some sort of meltdown be it returning to alcohol to take the edge off or quitting my business. Physically and mentally I would be on fire exiting that water. The rush of blood back to the skin creating a red glow, walking back to the car absolutely buzzing. It allowed me to take on whatever was thrown at me during this period. A simple 10 minute dip in cold sea water surrounded by like-minded people. Strangers the lot, from a different part of the world compared to Crossmolina. Some would chat, some would not.

Yet all warm folk there for different reasons, I am sure. It is a special spot and I love to return. Maybe its depth and ease make it so special. The life about both in the sea and on land. I am 1500 mtrs away from a body of water of a lake, but it does not seem to have the same dip qualities to draw me. Maybe it is the brown silty water that seems so dark and foreboding–I have gone for random dips whilst on long training runs which can be super special in various nooks and crannies of mountain lakes and streams about the wilds of the Nephin Wilderness Park. More than likely, the bathing and drinking site for millennia before me.

The Coombe was to be our second home for several months. Alma being released for the day depended on who was in charge as there was a genuine risk of infection.

Having PPROM really meant that this baby girl could come at any time, but at the same time being outside in the fresh air, the Forty Foot or the shops was very beneficial to her. Some allowed day release and saw the benefits of having a break. Some seemed more conservative in their dealings, which is fair.

Like day release from a prison, but the Coombe was far from a prison. To me, it became like a second home where you got to recognise staff and security and got to know all the midwives from different counties, countries and backgrounds. Getting to know other couples that we would never have socialised with or met previously. It all ground down to a very basic life. This had a bearing and still does. Expectant mothers and couples would come and go or come and stay. Some would lose their baby, some would hold on to their baby. It is a very fluid movement of life that seems to have its own course mapped out.

Taking Alma out on pretend dates, like we were a teenage couple back in the day going to the old Ballina Cinema. Holding hands, buying sweets. Simple. But now with so much more at stake, going to see "A Star is Born" together–an emotional roller coaster of a film for two in that cinema who were on a roller coaster as it was. I think we could have made a better choice. But it is an abiding memory all the same. Even the soundtrack brings me back. Exiting the film that day, I spotted Richie Sadlier. Being a second captains world service member at the time, I was going to say hello to him, but I didn't bother in the end. I think we were all shaken by what Bradley Cooper's character did. He was a sound buck. Recently, Richie Sadlier and his partner, who I didn't actually follow, came up in my Instagram feed. Showing an image of a baby at 22 weeks' gestation. He, they. Pretty much at the same point we were at all those years ago. I find the unconnected connections strange and amusing. Little did he know what was ahead of him. And that the guy staring at him thinking that he looks taller than he does on TV is going through something similar to what his future may bring. At the point of writing, I hope it works out for them all. I totally understood what they were saying and where they were at.

10. Dublin City Marathon 2018

We had many scares within this great big scare; we were at the mercy of amniotic fluid, which could lead to further bleeds and further stress to a baby, womb and all those connected. Firefighting one day at a time trying to allow Danny and Naoise some sort of normality with their mother was hard work, one of the worst images of many seared into my brain is when we were all waving bye to Alma one Sunday evening as she was flanked in between red bricked buildings of a south Dublin city street in mid-October. Sometimes bleeds would compete with timing whilst the kids were up to see their Mam for a weekend.

During this distressing situation, we were lucky enough to have Alma's cousin Brian and his partner Kevin available to babysit our other two whilst I sped back to the Coombe once more expecting some sort of delivery, as we were told it was code red with this babies heart rate now beginning to drop but nothing being delivered only further copious amounts of cortisol within our own bodies.

Meeting the Master-to-be of the Coombe this time around, he said that this baby would get to 32 weeks. It was another ward, another room, another group of highly specialised people doing their absolute best day in and day out of a week. Another scare came and went as all were stood down and a return to a normal ward for Alma with normal checks every few hours with her now Italian midwives. And back I went to a hotel room to relieve the latest group of people that were called in at late notice for a dig out.

The following week Ger Prendergast got in contact with me. He had recently won a Decaman, which is 10 Ironman distance triathlons every day for 10 days. I had given him my race entry for the 2018 Dublin City Marathon to be held the following weekend, as I thought when all went down that day in Castlebar there was no way I was going to race that particular years Dublin City Marathon.

Ger could not do the race, so I thought to myself, feck it sure I am in Dublin, anyway. It would be rude not to do it.

At this point, I had not really trained properly since late July, tapering for Ironman Estonia, just tipping away with the odd run if I had the time and maybe lifting a bit. I had put some off-season weight back on and was way out of the groove.

My old man said "sure you're fit".

And one would think that after completing an Ironman a few months previously, one is "fit". However, the reality of going to race in a marathon after a multi-month hiatus is a different story. I think it was all bravado, and the fact was that I was up in Dublin anyway with the race literally passing the Coombe. Considering everything, the break in training and periodisation, speed and endurance, a goal of 3 hours 30 minutes was set.

I love the Dublin marathon weekend. It is a real treat. I would usually spend €50 euro extra for a hotel that was not outside the M50 and closer to race start. One of those hotels that may have a knockoff Nespresso machine. High end stuff. You meet all the local runners, runners you have met over the years or what cracks me up runners that you met in nightclubs over the years. Men and women, capable of doing anything. But not capable of dealing with the aftermath now.

This year, of course, was different. I was staying with Mark and Yvonne in Swords and made my way into the city and parked in the Jurys Christchurch car park. I am early at the best of times, but for races normally I am one of the first people in. Ready or not ready in this instance, I can't lose that attitude somehow.

In a normal sense, considering the lack of a specific training phase for this race, I should have been a lot more nervous than I was. But there was more to it and that day the weather was glorious in the morning. I was racing for a bump now, as much as anything else. Still targeted and trying.

The Dublin Marathon winds its way around close to the halfway point at Dolphins Barn. The Coombe is just across the road. It's a very well supported race. Crowds line most of the road, cheering throughout. This is made even better when people from home will see you and shout for you. The crowds were several people deep, coming about the corner at the Coombe. I was hugging the left-hand side, staying right beside where the crowds were so I could see or hear Alma. But no sign and no sound.

Deep down I knew she would have been there if she could, she was bored out of her tree most of the time so the fact that the Dublin Marathon was literally running outside the hospital she was in, she would go for a look anyway. I felt that there were many people supporting me on the course from home so word would have gotten to me if she was going into labour or something was going down. So I kept going, but making sure to make eye contact with anyone from home along the way. All I got was encouragement rather than you need to get your ass back to the Coombe. So I just gave it my all to finish the final half of the race.

The discomfort in my feet is my most overriding memory of these latter stages of the race. The lack of training volume and training in the previous weeks had come to pass at the midway point. I came in a respectable 3:34. I did not hang around. I got my street wear bag and made my way to my car. Arriving back to Alma's hospital bed with a marathon medal for her bump only to find out she had a bleed and was in the high dependency unit attached to machines, so she could go nowhere that day.

Baby didn't arrive, it was Alma's third bleed of four in as many weeks; I guess she was numb to the outside world at this stage; it was all so close but yet so far as I said bye once more to her and a tiny bump and headed for a shower and sleep.

11. Code Red

During all this time, I would complete my classes at Strand Fitness. My clients are the best in the world spending their hard-earned cash on a fitness instructor that was constantly on edge. I don't really know how Billy Holland continued playing and performing as a professional rugby player for Munster. I was barely holding it together, never mind playing at the highest level with all eyes upon you coming home to relieve my mother, who minded Danny and Naoise to put them to bed and clean the house as mothers do. Every night without fail I would go to bed, rinse and repeat, as this was the way it went for 10 weeks in total.

But the night of the 7th of November 2018 was different. Alma called me at 10pm. "I'm going into labour, get up here safely please". Getting your shit together when your wife is going into labour can only be defined as code red level 10. After the journey from our 22-week scan to now 32-week labour, it was surreal. I got dressed and called my mother at the same time. Hitting the road, only stopping for a can of red bull to keep me tuned, thinking that I may make it up in time. Anyone that grew up driving in the late 90s around North Mayo and Mayo in general knows when and where to floor it. There are times when this is somewhat acceptable. And this was a time.

As light follows day, the Yin and Yang, the earth circling on its axis.

There was the fecking Garda with a speed camera at 10:30 pm outside Foxford. I was like, why? It's 10:30 pm. Why would you be there? Am I caught? Is he coming after me? Why is he not sounding the sirens and flashing his lights? A cat-and-mouse game between Foxford and Swinford, wondering if this Garda was going to pull me over or not. I had the story mentally rehearsed. Hoping that he had a couple of sprogs himself. Maybe his wife was pregnant. Maybe he is in a similar situation. Or maybe I have been reported. Driving like Miss Daisy with a squad car behind me on good quality albeit bendy roads. I waited in vain for this guy to make a move.

Thankfully, as I go to indicate left on the Padraig Flynn Road, he indicates right and heads towards Castlebar. There was a little bit of paranoia. Maybe he is fecking with me.

Maybe his Cheech is up behind the wooden wall in Charlestown, to which I waited, pumped with adrenaline and caffeine and no unmarked or marked car to be seen.

As Tommy Tiernan said, "Man, I fecking floored it", for about 10 mins.

I received a call from Nicola who just delivered our third baby. She delivered a baby girl. She delivered a baby that I was told was going to resemble a tadpole. A baby girl that we were told would not survive beyond a few weeks, if at all. Baby Dara was born bum and legs first as she quietly made her way into the delivery ward of the Coombe Hospital. The silence of delivery being quite hard on Alma.

I was told all was ok and to take my time coming up. Which I did. Upon arrival I made my way up to Alma who, although was tired and groggy, she was absolutely hyper. So hyper, I think she should have been given a sedative or something. Her eyes were bulging out of her head. I wanted to go see my baby, but we were told �not yet'. I did not understand this. I thought we were good to go. Baby is born, out the gap, let's get on with it. But I guess Dara, now all alone but not alone, had to do a little bit of scrapping by herself down there.

12. The Farney Man

Now delivered, I saw a different side of the Coombe. There was a whole different world on the other side of that door. One passed various levels of security and suited his or herself with various plastic garments to prevent infection. The Coombe was under partial renovation and felt like one was entering a spaceship lock and hallway upon opening a door. Here to the side of this building lay the NICU. Or at the end of the spaceship hall, lay the spaceship control centre where maybe up to 6 cocoon-like structures lay each with a tiny human baby inside. They were like 6 huge power banks that powered the entire Coombe Hospital and life.

Where our story began in a labyrinth–there felt a return to said labyrinth. Just another side of it. Maybe the inside.

Here our third child lay. Unable to hold, with UV light helping her yellow jaundice, she was so tiny in this great big cocoon of a machine. She was on a ventilator because she had pulmonary hypertension. We could stick our hands in and touch her. The size of my hand was about the same size as her.

She just lay there sleeping, oblivious to the world about her. Oblivious to the commotion, life or death. Maybe she was just concerned with her own breaths. We watched them, each one and the oxygen saturation levels associated with the same. Tiny but strong as an ox and paddling her own canoe. All by herself, with each breath, she grew stronger. Maybe I could hold her in a week or so.

It was here that I saw strength. Real strength. I have been around many a hard man both as part of Crossmolina GAA where players like Pat Mc Andrew with eyes and biceps bulging ready for championship games. Men that I used to look at as a 17-year-old and thank the gods that they were on our team. Men that would have made me shit myself on the championship grasses of Mayo. But as strong and as hard as they were, even they did not match the strength of the man from Monaghan.

As I sat in a waiting area, I was privy to a hallway conversation. Not for gossip or for news. I was just there, and this was a common story. Here this Monaghan man, without a quiver or break in his voice, with poise and strength and a definite course of action, told his boy without once welling that this boy's brother and his son would not live. He told his son that he would say bye to his little brother and they could not watch premier league matches together. This dad with his stoney grey soil accent (Kavanagh) was a tower of strength, a wall that has stood the test of time. I listened and commended him internally for his unbelievably steadfast nature of delivery. He was a dad doing a dad's job. Holding the ship together.

There were some surreal moments too. I observed a male nurse whom I call the Portuguese Mo Salah as he looked like the King of the Kop. He moved about the NICU whilst singing. As he moved from cocoon to cocoon, he would sing.

"Don't blame it on the moonlight,
don't blame it on the good times,
blame it on the boogie."

I would watch him bound about, momentarily checking stats and sats and then move off again in verse and rhyme. All the other staff seemed to be so used to him and loved him dearly. I suppose it makes sense that one would have to have such a make-up and demeanour to work in what seemed a flip of a coin to life and death. Where in the same week, a twin passed but his/her brother or sister lived. Some babies made it through, whilst others did not. Some parents were elated and beginning to move on and grow with their lives, whilst others were falling apart from the inside.

One wondered if there was a God and why such a God favoured some over others. Or was this just the great big spinning wheel of life? With Monaghan man and Portuguese Mo Salah, I think of them regularly. I think about them in those halls where doctors and nurses scurried about that great spaceship performing miracles and suffering catastrophic loss.

13. Hugh's House

We are not the first couple or lone parent to beat this path. To wear the halls, to worry, to make it all work. Not the first to kip on couches or get a room from friends. It's a great country until there is a problem where all roads lead to our Rome, or in this case, Dublin. Not living a commutable distance owing to the perennial lack of infrastructure and services which may stay the same for generations to come, one needs the help of friends.

A few years previously, a Dublin couple had observed what those from the country were experiencing trying to make things work. They saw them sleeping on chairs and couches, trying to secure accommodation in hotels and B and B's. The expense and the stress. So they did something about it. They invested in a red-bricked terraced house just off Mountjoy Square in Dublin 1 and made this ancient house a home for many of the individuals and couples going through their own personal turmoil in any of the maternity hospitals in Dublin.

As Alma had delivered Dara, she needed somewhere to stay for a further four weeks. We were introduced to and told about this amazing place that Alma could stay in until Dara could be transferred down to the west of Ireland. Hugh was a baby that had passed on and they named this house after him.

Oh my word, was it a special place. They were renovating the space as we were there in that period. People were writing their stories on the walls that were soon to be papered, painted, or built over. The ancient house where thousands of people would have passed through in this ancient part of the city was alive. It was alive with the spirits of those who had passed and it was alive with the spirit of life of those that lived there and wanted their little ones to live and be healthy. Taking a selfie photo of myself and Danny in a mirror placed in the highest upstairs room, whether a trick of light or not, one can clearly see a light about my hand. Such was the level of spirit that was contained here in these homely and comfortable rooms.

It gave Alma a wonderful home whilst in Dublin, and it gave us great peace of mind. Having now decided that I along with 3 others would pay a £500 deposit towards the

Marathon Des Sables, the toughest foot race in the world to be held in 2020, I said I would use it as a platform to raise funds for the Hugh's House charity. Which is one of the most amazing places for parents going through the worst things imaginable. Alma stayed here until we were all strong enough to be transferred back down to Castlebar in December 2018, where baby Dara was to spend a further two weeks in SCBU.

Now closer to home, I could spend more time and get to know my little one. She could still fit comfortably in one of my hands. But with each day she grew stronger, and with Christmas looming, we could bring baby Dara home and unite our family once more under the one roof on December 19th, 2018.

14. 100km Race Attempt

Life returned to some sort of normality, albeit like many. Our house was absolutely bat shit crazy. Dara Drama Loftus came home in a Pavlik harness as she was born breach and her hip was dislocated, which is quite common with premature babies. Because of this, she was referred to Crumlin Hospital in Dublin which invariably meant that Alma would take care of these appointments where I would hold the fort at home, and by holding the fort I mean my mother would actually hold the fort whereas I was there on some sort of consultancy basis.

Dara needed to have an operation on her hip called a ‘closed reduction’. The first operation failed and Alma found it quite traumatic holding her when she was being put under for the operation, and then she came out with a cannula in her head which did not help her anxiety either. We realised after further x-rays two weeks post operation that the closed reduction operation had failed as her hip came back out, so Alma and Dara went back to Crumlin a further two weeks later for a second operation. This time without a cannula in the head and the second operation was a success where Dara was put in a second spica cast, which immobilised her lower body but had an opening for changing nappies.

She had 3 spica casts over the following 4 months that matched her size. I pulled a fast one, stating that my huge manly hands were too big to change the nappies in the spica casts. It was all going great until Alma met a bigger man from Co. Roscommon in Crumlin Hospital who did not have the same problem. Goes to show that Roscommon men have to ruin everything for Mayo men! It is part of their genetic make-up! Luckily, this was towards the end of all the casts, so I had dodged an enormous amount of situations with my supposed huge manly hands that were too enormous to change spica cast based nappies.

Thereafter, Dara went into a Rhino brace for a further 3 months. Life was getting a little easier bit by bit but as you can imagine every now and again, there would be absolute logistical meltdowns such as Naoise’s fondness towards the staff at Castlebar A&E. She had started playschool and was becoming quite active and with that, also quite accident prone. Also, with Danny now in Crossmolina National School, we seemed to be just on the road all the time.

Dara's hips still needed work, and having had so many x-rays, the images of the ball and socket hip joint are seared into my brain at various stages along the way. These things obviously take time and it was hard to be patient. With time and movement, this being the best thing for bone growth, our belief in her also began to grow, but biannual visits to Crumlin Hospital were still a little stressful knowing that there are other issues that need to be resolved.

Life was crazy but somehow we all got into a stride with careers, study, and training for the 2020 Marathon Des Sables. In preparation for the race, I had signed up for my first 100km distance race that was to be held in Ballina in February 2020. Cezary Lubinski and his partner Daria, members of Ireland's Marathon club which organise and race marathons all over the country organised this race. They are an extremely eclectic bunch. The race was an out- and-back along the rolling back roads to Killala twice, around Beleek Woods in Ballina and then the balance of the race comprised laps of a 1 mile lit loop in Beleek for safety as towards the latter stages of the race it would be dark.

I was in great shape at the time and was doing well however; the weather was absolutely atrocious. The northwest of Ireland was experiencing storm Jorge. My nutrition at the time was Muertan sachets that I would add to my water bottles. It froze a bit in the bottles and became stuck in the straw. With the drop in temperature during the race, I think I got a little bit of hyperthermia as I needed help to fill my bottles. Yet, I was still doing well in the race, a good bit behind the race leader but still in the top 5 position. This was awesome for me. Then the heavens opened further, the winds became gale force and the temperature plummeted. At about 40 odd kilometres for me, the race was actually called off because of safety concerns.

With the race now cancelled and participants making their way off the course, I kept going and do the distance myself. I was feeling good and was operating on my free-will, running on public roads and grounds, so there was no problem. I was raising money for Hugh's House at the time and I went online while I was running, explaining the craic on Instagram and Facebook. Then, low and behold, loads of money started flowing in as people got behind the madness and contributed towards our go fund me account for Hugh's House. Thousands were taken in that day, which was awesome and it really made all the madness worthwhile. Alma and the kids came in with coffee and fig rolls, the nutrition of champions, as did my parents at a later stage–I can still remember the apple lattice they brought for me! The hot coffees really helped as I knocked out 50 kms, then 60 kms, making my way onto the 1 mile looped track.

Anyone that knows my running style and training knows that I dislike or do small loops. They do my head in. I would sooner do one big loop be that 10, 20, 30,40, 50 kms in training rather than any combination of small loops. But out of nowhere, one of my training buddies, Aiden O' Donnell, came into Beleek, Ballina and started running with me. At this stage, however, my run was starting to turn into a run, walk, shuffle, run because of the effects of it getting cold earlier on that day. Aiden coached another 10 kilometres out of me, now bringing my total for the day and my personal best run distance at 70 kms, 8 hours 23 minutes. I called it a day, as there was nothing else to prove, only my madness.

What started out as a great opportunity to race ended up being a disaster with the weather, but this disaster was great in raising funds for Hugh's House. I don't think I would have raised €1,450.00 that day without Storm Jorge, which was a fantastic and very positive ending to one of the wettest and coldest days of 2020.

15. The COVID 2km Radius Marathon

Soon after the race I was quite sick with some sort of chest issue. Nothing would seem to shake. That was February 2020! Worlds were falling apart for me, my business and what was a race I had been preparing for since November 2018. I was coming into a taper for the Marathon Des Sables with all my training now completed and gear ready to rock and roll. Then essentially, boom!!! a race supposed to start in March 2020, in the middle of what was a total meltdown, also known as Covid-19, all was called off and pushed out until September 2020.

I did not have the support of tent mates. Those that had initially signed up and put deposits down had long since pulled out. I was in an online world of Facebook groups that got really shitty and nasty. Everyone was simply speculating, because nobody knew back then what was going on and how long it would go on for.

They reduced us to a 2km radius distance of movement that April 2020! With the Marathon Des Sables now cancelled I wanted to draw a line under the fundraising for Hugh's House as I did not know what was going to happen with the actual race and obviously did not want money "resting in my account" via GoFundMe so I decided I would do a Marathon distance race 42.2km in a time trial format within our own 2km radius on my own. We were lucky that we lived on a loop around Crossmolina, so it worked out perfectly.

Alma and the kids could watch on from the garden as I ran around the 2km radius, Dara now able to stand up and watch herself with the aid of a stroller, with the other two bombing around the garden during what was beautiful weather. I encouraged those that come to Strand Fitness and beyond to join me virtually as I did 8 loops of our then radius.

As always, I started out way too fast and blew up along the way, struggling on the last 10 kms but as a time trial for 42.2 kms, it was not bad going for 3 hours and 31 minutes. If I started out a bit easier, I could maybe have done better. To be honest, once I got going I found it to be very akin to racing against others even though I was just racing against the clock or watch in this case. Psychologically, I was very focused on the present, that being whatever part I was on or had to navigate rather than the bigger picture of the day itself. Which would be very similar for me and any race. It was enjoyable even with my customary blow up, maybe because I had done so much training and this effort was the culmination of all that training and investment, both physically and mentally.

The race gave a final push for raising funds for Hugh's House where our final total was €5,375 and also with all the online posting a certain Crossmolina man Richard raised a further €4,000 through his technology company that was transferred directly to Hugh's House. So not a bad effort on everyone's part and I am forever grateful.

We still have not gone back to Dublin to meet with the management and staff of Hugh's House to date but I know that Ade and Robert have effectively used the donations and mothers and fathers are benefiting from this service as life simply goes on.

We look forward to returning as a family. I am sure it will be a very emotional time for us, all going back to that ancient part of Dublin 1.

16. The Kingdom's Apprenticeship

Having signed up in 2018 to do an April 2020 race, that I completed it in 2023 is mad in itself. They cancelled Marathon Des Sables in 2020 when we were in the throes of COVID. It was postponed to September 2020 and then again to 2021. I had raised €5,375 euros in the lead up to the 2020 race and just transferred the cash to the Hugh's House team as I did not want to have the money resting in my account Fr. Ted style until I had actually completed the race. Training again for the same race only to be postponed again (September 2020), I opted to change my race to 2023 thinking at the time whatever is going on, it should be resolved by then. In preparations, I had gone through nearly every emotion and after the mess of the 2021 edition, where there was a bug in camp and with one competitor sadly dying. I tried to pull a fast one to get some or all of the entry monies paid, which is about the €6,000 mark. As the October 2021 edition came across as really messy, with loads complaining on the online groups, coupled with a Guardian article about all the issues that were encountered because of the bug in the camp and the subsequent breakdown in management of the race itself, I was not really all that enthused about the race anymore. I wanted nothing to do with it, really. There was a lot of money invested, but with all that had gone on with COVID also, it was nearly ok to have a bad debt situation with something like this. Many agreed that I should just pull the pin on it. A cousin of mine who knew previous competitors even said that it was not really all it was cracked up to be.

The company that organises the UK and Irish runners called my bluff in the end, and of course, I at the time preferred to do something I did not want to do as I had paid the money for it. And if I paid all that dough, by jaysus, I was going to enjoy it. Now, I have come full circle and am very glad that my bluff was called. Even though this race has dragged on for years with its stop start nature, and I am sure everyone is sick of hearing about it. I am sick of talking about it too. And just want to go and get it done. 2020 seems like such a long time ago. I would have completed the race, no doubt. However, I think I am a more rounded ultra-runner now. Those three years have matured my running. In those years I did a few races of the Kerry way ultra-series. The first the Kerry Way Lite 58km in September 2020, the Kerry Way Ultra 200km in September 2021 and the Kerry Way Ultra Nite in September 2022.

For all the training I have done over the last 5 years, I think these races have taught me the most about ultra-running and, in a way, myself. The Lite is a wonderful race and I would recommend anyone wishing to do an ultra to give it a go. It's long enough to challenge you but short enough not to kill you. I came in at a respectable 15th place which would be good for me, and I was delighted at the time.

The greatest learning, however, came with my greatest failure. That was the 2021 200km edition. Looking back now, I was way overconfident to think I could complete this race in the way I intended to do it. Off my head even. Coupled with the fact that I was not feeling the best on the way down to Kerry. One of those non covid respiratory infections that would not simply feck off. I had hoped to literally run it out of me in the first quarter of the race.

200kms is a long way, 200kms along the Kerry way is a long way on crack. What I was thinking standing on that start line will always be one of my personal mysteries. I was not in the best of form, not really wanting to mix or chat. The start of these races are very chatty and friendly. Because they are so long unless you are the top 10%, there really is not any point in going off like a headless chicken so conversations are struck up and friendships are made. It's lovely really.

I was in no form for chatting and felt quite dead. This coupled with a girl who went for a dump pretty much on the trail ordering me "Not to look" at her having a poop. I thought, I'm really not into this sort of thing and why could you not go 20 metres in any fecking direction downwind for your dump.

We then awkwardly ran close to each other around the black valley. Not awkward at all. That's ultrarunning. Waiting for a gear to kick in that never kicked in, trying to enjoy what is a wonderful experience as you run through areas that many just simply do not know exist. But I was in the horrors very early on, barely able to descend, wondering what the feck was wrong with me.

Meeting Alma at the first marathon point, she knew I was not in a good place. I tried to eat in the hope it would help. Tried podcasts but I was hardly listening. The hills and mountains at this stage are pretty undulating. I met Alma again and even though I said I was not feeling it, I said I would try to get to Foilmore.

Arriving into Foilmore, one can see the local GAA pitch well into the distance. I knew my race was over. When one's head is gone, it is gone. There is not much that can be said or done to resurrect the situation. Alma even had Mayo Ladies, Geelong and Galway United superstar Rachel Kearns call me to get me going again. Unfortunately, I was goosed. I just wanted to quit and go to bed. I had bitten off way more than I could chew and I knew it deep down I was way out of my Ultra league. Sitting on a camping chair feeling sorry for myself, I actually had a little snooze. Alma, who had befriended many of the competitors teams received some expert advice about not letting me quit straight away. Giving me some time to really want to quit. My mind was made up hours earlier on the ascent to Drum hill. As beautiful as it was and as amazing as Kerry is, it did nothing for my mindset. Alma tried in vain once more, but I was done. Nearly embarrassed, I just wanted to get away from Foilmore, away from all the other real athletes and their support teams. I just wanted to go to bed. After 77kms and 13 hours of racing, I did just that.

I spent a fair bit of time with my tail firmly between my legs, and of course I did what many do here. Try to put things right, so I resigned up to the following year's 2022 Kerry Way Ultra 200kms once more. Thinking that it would have me in good stead for the desert in 2023 and also to put things right and not be beaten by the course and thus Kerry.

My coach Stephen was not too enthused about the idea of another rattle at the 200kms course. He thought, and rightly so, if it did not work out once more I would be in a very dark place preparing for the toughest race of my life and the toughest foot race on earth.

Therefore, I emailed the lovely Eileen in Killarney and asked to be dropped back to do the 100km Nite run for September 2022, which makes up over half of the long course. I had never raced at night before. It was a totally different experience that was not even dampened by the heavens opening up in the lead up to race start just outside of Waterville.

Starting just after the sun had set, headlamps were turned on and myself and Foxford man Colin Dockery snaked our way through fields and hedgerows on and off the Kerry way. It turned out to be a really beautiful night. Starting out quite mild but getting colder around the really dark hours. It amazed me at how natural it was to be running and racing in the late hours. As a race it was quite special, the moon danced up the hills in front of you on the way back into Waterville, much like the head of a creamy pint of Guinness, at points the moon was huge as it stared and danced as I bounced from rock to rock. Kerry is a special part of the world, but at night and even in the pitch of dark, it is even more special. Amazed at the temperature changes that could be felt throughout at different stages. The course is extremely mountainous but for the most part, I really enjoyed running where I could and hiking where I had to. Passing through Caherdaniel, Sneem and on towards Kenmare as darkness moved towards light, I was actually doing quite well. I had a pain in my hip which I know now was the start of a lot of IT band and hip issues I was lucky to borrow Colins crew for the night, Tadhg Duffy, who was a great help and had some pain killers with him which helped me get through the middle section of the race as I was in a fair bit of pain.

Even through the night Alma lay awake in her bed throughout the small hours messaging me about my race position and how I was doing compared to the other runners, as I was still competitive at that point, hoping for a fairly decent placing.

Arriving into Kenmare with only about 18 kilometres to the finish line, I thought all the hard work was done. There is a really tough hill outside of Kenmare. It just goes up and up, and then up some more. I knew what it was and what it consisted of. I knew what was ahead of me and what I needed to do to finish the race out. But my god did I bonk like I have never bonked before.

Once I reached the summit of that final hard hill and into what are the handy trails of Kerry national park my body and mind totally broke down. Tourists were taking photos of me like I was some sort of zoo animal. I was that bad. My head was totally gone. The only way to quit was to call in the Kerry Mountain Rescue Team. Can one imagine the embarrassment? A rescue team calling upon a smelly bonking Ultra Runner.

The only option was to keep going. Each step was murderous and I only had myself to blame, making a mess of my nutrition towards the latter stages of the race. Feeling so sorry for myself and focusing way too inwardly, the heavens decided to open up once more as I finally made it into Torc waterfall after about two hours.

One descends from Torc Waterfall into Muckross House, which may as well be a maze or a time warp. I was close, but I may as well have been in the Azores. It took approximately a further hour to get from Muckross to the Killarney Racecourse where I completed the race of 103.5 kms in 18 hours and 29 minutes.

I was supposed to have a sleeping in the back of my car and then hit the road back to Mayo. That turned into having a snooze in the car and booking a hotel room for the night. I was in a total hoop.

Looking back now, it was this experience that really stood to me. I think for some; it is very important to endure this level of suffering to prepare for something bigger or harder. I soon realised that pushing through those 18 kilometres was probably the best training I had done from a mental standpoint. With absolutely nothing left in the tank and a considerable distance left to go, I could simply just keep going. I learned personally what is still possible and I also learned that I needed to work on being more positive in these situations if they arise in the future. One does not have to be negative when there is nothing left.

The greatest learning from all these races, as cliché as it sounds, is the ability to remain as positive as possible for as long as possible. I have noticed that a lot of the Irish finishers, both male and female, in these races seem to be happy during the race. They may suffer internally, but it does not seem to show outwardly. Many of the finishers who may not be the top 5% also possess this ability to be positive. This cliché really has a positive effect that is needed in these distances and severity of courses.

Being negative, feeling sorry for oneself, being negative in one's thoughts chips away at one's ability to complete these extreme events. It just simply does not work. Those that finished before the allotted 40 hours may not have done more training than me. But between their ears, they were certainly in a better place than me. And I was very aware of this, leaving Killarney the next morning with my tail between my legs. Again.

I made a mental note to simply love the grind more. Even more than I thought I already did. Even though I have made many changes over the years from smoking cessation, alcohol cessation and a more veganish lifestyle I sought to create more time for recovery and thankfully was introduced to Dr Joe Dispenza's meditations and Jocko Willinks' discipline equals freedom mindset, among many other people, influences and strategies.

Actively working on being more positive during a race was probably one of my greatest learnings over the last 15 years of endurance-based racing.

17. On The Sand Road Again

I love autumn as the surf is so good. I don't have any college work for a few months and I can recharge for the following season. Surfing more has become a focus for mindset and wellness. There is so much going on, especially when it is busy, that there is absolutely nothing else going on in my head other than what I am experiencing there and then. Thus I am surfing. I am in the present moment. I am there wherever there is, and I am nowhere else mentally. I am not daydreaming, drifting, thinking about errands or chores to do. I have my eyes on the horizon or positioning myself in a lineup and back on the horizon again. Scanning the water, scanning people, scanning the waves.

Truth be told, considering I have been surfing since the early noughties when it boomed back then, I’m pretty shit. Having not gotten lessons and developing the worst drop knee pop up imaginable coupled to wanting to surf shorter boards too early, I shafted my growth and held myself back. Only now in my mid 40s am I starting to progress.

I was scared shitless of surfing on my own for a long time but wanting to get better and improve I worked hard with my S and C coach and essentially made myself ‘man up’ and get in the water on my own as often as possible.

Now I don’t enjoy surfing with anyone! I prefer to nip off at first light and be getting out of the water when others are getting in. I am in no ways surfing anyway credibly. The term would be intermediate and not to make a bollox of myself. But I have some of the most amazing moments that leave me higher than any drug can could do.

I made the most of the autumn and winter of 2022 surfing 2/3 times per week if possible, memory banking one or two of the best waves I have caught over the last 20 years. It helps my running, be it recovery in the water, using different muscle groups or just simply watching the early morning sunlight illuminate a wave in the darkest parts of winter.

Like an analgesic effect. Just being there, being present works. With my goofy poor pop up I can sometimes angle the odd, amazing moment. Being helped onto the board through caring and/ or uncaring reef breaks depending on the location, one can feel the most amazing levels of bliss as you can feel tonnes of water funnel under your feet. With more boards than I need, one is chosen based on any given day's feeling of confidence. All loaded with volume whilst I get in the way of the artistic Cain Killcullens of this world. Every now and again, that moment is delivered. Sometimes shocked at my own very location on a wave for a few fleeting moments, I can get the 101 basics right and go rail to rail. On the better days whooped on by the local contingent. That always makes it feel, oh, so much better. The added elation is a bonus on top of the already overflowing levels of dopamine flowing from this rush of feeling by riding nature as hard and as fast until the invariable smash. No kudos or coolness existing without any real style. But it does not matter being buried under a few feet of water smiling so much internally that even the frowns and sneers from style merchants can't dampen the squid smiling inside of me.

Front loading the week with salt water if the charts allowed with longer more energy sapping runs towards the latter stages of the week. It is, of course, possible to do the two on the one day. With my brother Niall up for a rare session over Christmas 2022, I ran 27 kms in the early morning and get a session in with him later that day. With loads of day trippers down, holiday vibes and the place firing, it was probably not a great idea. But it shows what is possible once one is motivated.

Training gradually increases. Most of the time, it's like being in a holding pattern waiting for air traffic control to allow you to land. Then once the go ahead is given, you can feel that schedule begins to fill. There are less easy days and more double days. Being able to squeeze in a surf after a run is seen as a bonus 12 weeks out there is nothing easy about a double run day that I sneakily subbed for a 22 kilometre 5am run instead. Forgiveness is better than permission. My coach Stephen was not happy but the thoughts of a double run on a workday having to be Mr Motivator for my clients did not appeal to me.

But once layered up with a base layer, technical tee, light rain jacket and a run bag with some nutrition and water, I am good to go. Once these runs start getting longer and longer, all those podcasts that were put on the long finger get a listen to. Everything from Tim Ferris, Rich Roll, Jocko Willink, David Mc Williams, The Surfers Journal, and the Irish History podcast and everything else in between. The hours of podcasts listened to and subjects covered. If only it was like a Matrix scenario where all the information would be delivered to stick inside my head. Deep topics, history, business, economics. Whatever the flavour of the day, there is so much information to consume yet hard to hold on to. Sometimes I may have several tit bits, random pieces of information of the most banal things. For the most part, people's stories seem to be the most enjoyable to listen to. How people walked from Mayo to Dublin starving with green lips during the famine to climb aboard coffin ships. Reading about the Famine in North Mayo would leave a level of spook as to those that lay on ditches on the very same roads that I now traversed. Fr. Hoban's "On Our Knees" stories of local townlands making it all so related. The statistics showing percentages lost when those statistics for any given townland were hundreds to thousands. Here lies something that many city dwellers would not realise about running in the likes of Mayo. Hop scotching from townland to townland in order to move parish to parish or town to town. Each townland, that may look like a group of fields to an outsider, has its own mini culture and vibe, history and sense of being, but still relatively poorly known compared to the streets and avenues worn by runners in Dublin, Cork, Limerick and Galway. The names make sense like Fairfield or Rathduff but some need deeper exploration and meaning. Each having their own personality.

On the road again, sometimes mixing podcasts for music, big Americana works great as does anything from Ludovico Einauidi to the Gloaming. Anything that allows the mind to wander in the space. Sometimes running, one can become emotional. Sometimes music will open that up and allow you to embrace that inner part of self that wants to release and feel. To let go even.

Being on the road again to a race is great. It focuses and gives me a sense of direction. Getting these sessions done early gives each day an early win and a sense of achievement. Rising for the bulk of the training season at 4:59am. That minute for my ego as if I am getting up at 4am. Jocko Willink inspires it. Discipline equals freedom. The discipline to get up and get it done. That even when somewhat fatigued, I still always feel great. Finishing up when others are beginning their own personal rat race. Car lights beaming and streaming in the distance towards bigger towns and jobs.

Being done, the feeling of accomplishment every morning is awesome. Sometimes a double session strength and conditioning and a run of various distances or a standalone run. It was all done whilst my wife and kids lay in their beds asleep. Sometimes Danny, Naoise or Dara would play musical beds moving from one room to the next until they were totally happy with that particular nights sleeping arrangement, slipping off like a ninja Dad, with all my kit laid out the night before, runners, socks, shorts, tops, nutrition, head torch and water. Only the hum of my Nespresso machine would sound in our very porous house. Give me caffeine and I can do anything.

Somehow come 4pm, sometimes with the aid of a nap, anything from 20 minutes to an hour, I am ready to go again and motivate those coming into Strand Fitness for their evening classes to get moving and working out during the tougher months of winter.

This winter seemed to be tougher than most, for a plethora of reasons. Maybe the post COVID adrenaline had run off, but folks seemed to be a bit edgier than normal. With just normal life now and no restrictions to contend with many seem to find the return to normal brass tacks hard to fathom or maintain. I do not mind the absolute blackness of winter, in fact I like it, for others the seasonal change short evenings and darker mornings are beyond difficult, there is no way of sugar coating or selling any sort of extra-curricular experience in the darkness, some can do it, but many cannot, and I felt sorry for those that cannot face it. They may resent winter lovers in a sense. Between darkness and cold water, I believe there is so much to love. Training as always before the rivers of car lights illuminate the roads may not be as effective to some as the blue skies of June but this early morning movement does help and it sets up my day, every day, this year the post-Christmas period was a grind for me training wise however, it was really tough for some people in other ways.

The other ways are the understanding now with age and the movement of time regarding the amount of men of all ages that stare into the blackness of water that sometimes is only illuminated by the yellow street lights that keep a watching eye over this flow. This flow along with the numbers that observe its wake is greatly underestimated, these estimations are leaving a trail of destruction behind because no one seems to have any sort of handle on what is actually going on with males about the latitude of geography where we all live. My run programming kept progressing, but these progressions were intertwined with flashing blue lights and the now movements of search parties.

How bad it must be for these souls to seek refuge there. With those intertwined days I spent mornings shining lights into the blackness, double jobbing. As were an entire community. On different crafts and using different devices. A coming together, but in sad circumstances. How nice it would be just to float in better circumstances. The struggle weighing greatly on the eyes and faces. A struggle for those to get through each day.

The first man up in the morning hammering the roads I spent those weeks like many glaring my head torch and peering over ditches and walls, it was incredibly solemn with people I knew and did not know trying to keep the strings of life together under incredible strain, thankfully I could run under the cover of darkness as to do so under light on these roads under these times would have been incredibly disrespectful. Days ran into the weekend, and the weekend was left behind for searching to continue for weeks whilst an entire community and communities from voluntary to professional did their bit.

Once this particular cloud was lifted another one filtered in behind, on the same day a family and friends were relieved only for a second group of family and friends to be destroyed with sadness, the crossing paths of it all was not lost on me, I knew neither man personally but like any community all within it feel some sort of an effect of a loss like this. A village raises a child and it certainly feels the loss of one also, with no easy answers or solutions, day follows night and many like myself keep doing what we are doing which must be just as hard for all those directly affected to observe, time moves on, and all I could do was offer cold water dips to help show the benefit of this freeze on the body, mind and spirit. I advertised it on my socials to entice a certain cohort, but only a small group of us would meet up locally and get into the lake for a cold dip in fresh water that January and February. It is a more positive way of using a static flow of water that seems to be lost on many who have not tried it. The most that need it never seem to come, instead they continue to suffer internally with an outward smile, it is not the solution by any means, but it is a tool in what is now an ever-growing tool box of solutions to help people of all ages wash off that black dog if even only for a few hours.

18. Final Build Block, Again

Even though I have been training for this race on and off for the guts of 5 years, the specific build block was quite tough. My coach, Stephen, adds training sessions via WhatsApp for two weeks at a time. Whatever he posts, I do. Simple as. Having joined the Jocko Willink Discipline Equals Freedom from afar, I found it to be of huge benefit to be able to rise before 5 am and get whatever session needed to be done. Done, before Alma and the kids rose and busy family days began.

These extra hours in the morning would allow me to do anything from driving the 20 minutes back to the hills in

Keenagh and completing a 16-kilometre run in the Dark Skies National Park to making it into Ballina for a track session, simple runs about Crossmolina and longer runs at the weekends.

January and February were quite mild, but it seemed to rain so much in March and April. Arriving back to park up at Keenagh Church with its solitary light illuminating the rain as it crashed sideways against it was always horrible. But I would be grand once I got going.

From mid-January I developed IT band issues, which is simply an overuse injury. The muscle is long and flat and goes down the side of one's thigh. It can cause pain in many parts of the upper leg but also cause pain below the knee. It is a common running injury and a really annoying one at that. One can be fine during one long run day and in agony the next. And like most runners, we hope that these injuries will just magically go away. Stephen shared a good stretch for it I would do in the middle of the road early in the mornings to elicit some sort of relief. Some days I came back in agony into the kitchen or sitting room trying to stretch whilst taking in vegan protein recovery drinks. I spent a considerable amount of time researching and working on gluteal and abduction exercises. Anything to take the pressure off what was becoming a huge problem. With physio appointments scarce, it was a student physio from Ardagh, Lee Traynor, who gave me an exercise that I would have never thought of that seemed to do the trick.

My lower back would also flare up badly once I ran past 30 kilometres. It's one of those funny back injuries that is not serious but quite debilitating. Physio, John Courell, had prescribed Jefferson Curls a year previously. If I do not stay on top of them within a few weeks, my back and body know about it. I do them as part of my strength and conditioning warm until sometimes I get lazy. Also possibly because of COVID, the Marathon Des Sables has dragged on so much and I may have taken a longer period off to rest these types of injuries, as many were simply overuse.

It felt like firefighting sometimes, trying to appease the body in different ways, but I was very focused in what I had to do. I think this focus manifested itself when I went to my dentist, Bernard, with a problematic tooth. This tooth had been a pain in the ass for years. After several fillings and coming and going, I had enough with this tooth as I felt it was not a team player. I reasoned I did not want to have a situation in the middle of the desert where I could have had a toothache. So, over a consultation with Bernard, I decided I wanted him to take that tooth out.

Others may think this is sick. But it made total sense to me. All I was thinking about was the completion of this race and anything that was not helping, both internally or externally, had to go. Like an artist at work, that molar was whipped out. I took a few days off training to avoid infection or any issues. I had dry socket but after a week I was back running again and happy to have that tooth in a bag at my work desk rather than in my mouth.

To be honest, at the time I thought nothing of it, but looking back now, I can see how focused I was on making sure I did everything possible to get to that finish line. I would have removed more teeth If I had to.

I think the run block I did in this period was one of the toughest that I have ever completed. It peaked at 115 to 120 kilometres per week. It's probably more fitting family, life, work and everything else around the block of training that makes it so hard and fatiguing. Weekends would include a double day which I absolutely detest. I would sooner run 40 kilometres early than 2 x 20 kilometres one early and one late. It created a 3-session weekend which is absolutely brilliant for training for such an event as the Marathon Des Sables but it does not make it anyway enjoyable. Getting up on a Sunday morning running for a few hours, going to train the Ardagh lads–home do some family stuff, i.e. watch cartoons with the kids and then back out again that afternoon and evening and repeat.

It would get to the stage where I would dream about running. I had a recurring dream about a fox and a deer chasing each other around Ballycarroon where "Wild Mountain Thyme" was filmed. In my dream it was pitch dark bar the outline of trees and ditches and this fox would chase a deer. I would often see a fox on my runs here along with a Barn owl close by with huge eyes on dark winters mornings. There were not many roads around Crossmolina that I did not touch. Running into neighbouring parishes and towns, I would get looks and shakes of the head as to places they could find me with one local man, Sean Keane, pulling over one day to tell me, "Jaysus, you could meet you anywhere."

I would grow fond then bored of a loop or group of loops and then move off in a different direction for a few weeks. Still always going for 20, 30, 40 kilometre loops rather than smaller ones. I preferred to carry provisions on my back such as water and fodder rather than loop back to my house or car. Sometimes I would loop through or around Killmurray Church and graveyard where our friend Brendan Heffernan was buried. He was killed in a motorcycle accident during Covid and we miss him greatly. Sometimes I would run up to his grave, sit down and put my earphones on his grave so whatever was there underneath could hear some tunes. Sometimes I would say “hello” but I rarely talked to him. I just sat there letting Heff listen to some music and then I would be on my way again.

As the race grew closer, our kids started getting sick. One by one they dropped with whatever was going in creches or schools. There was no avoiding it. Naoise, who is normally so resilient to anything, got some sort of virus and was absolutely floored. The others, including Alma, got sick but not as bad as Naoise. Whatever Naoise had, I soon picked up. Thinking as always, this would probably be just a 24/48 hour thing. I was actually quite sick and so angry that here I was, 2 weeks out from the toughest race of my life feeling like shit. I threw everything at it. It would go up and down, in and out. No sooner did I feel better than I got a sore throat again. I made a final trip into Molloy’s Pharmacy beside Strand Fitness and got everything that could be thrown at it, hearing in the process that it was a 10-day thing. I was literally leaving on the tenth day. There was no doubt I was going, irrespective of how I felt. Thankfully, as it became time to pack, I was feeling better. Alma had to listen to many meltdowns, though, in the lead up.

The drive to Knock was probably the tensest drive I have ever had with Alma. We brought Dara for good measure, leaving the other two in school. I was not bringing a phone during the race to save weight. But also, I really wanted to get off the grid and totally focus on what I was doing. I didn't want to hear about somebody who died at home whilst I was away. Albeit, that did not stop my brother Niall from emailing me about someone who died. I still don't know who it was that died.

During that tense car journey to Knock Airport I just kept repeating in my head, "Keep your mouth shut and say nothing", as I had the absolute fear that I would say the wrong thing. I promised to email when and where I could. The email service was great and the organisation would hand deliver emails to tents as well.

As the saying goes in Ballina, "I'll not give any guarantees", to which I held firm. I said I would email when and where I could. I like to under promise at the best of times and this was definitely one of those instances that needed under promising.

I left Alma and Dara at Knock Departures and was finally on my way to the 37th edition of the Marathon Des Sables.

Top Left: Alma feeding baby Dara in the Coombe
Top Right: Alma holding baby Dara Mayo General Hospital Dec 2018
Bottom Left: Barry kissing baby Dara in Mayo Genreal Hospital 5th Dec 2018
Bottom Right: Barry, Dara and Alma in the Coombe

Top and Middle: First day holding baby Dara
Bottom: Family at home in Crossmolina December 2018

Top: Barry with fellow Mayo race contestant, Alan
Middle: The author in the Sahara desert race May 2023
Bottom: Remaining Tent 80 Race Crew in the Sahara Desert May 2023

The Sahara

19. Marathon Des Sables Arrival, Finally

Arriving in the desert in a convoy of buses, we passed a house mocked up to look like a western American cowboy and Indian style farmstead complete with a ploughed brown field which was surrounded by a fence similar to any I have seen in various films of the American 1800s period. With all the woodwork of the house and porch carefully put together but rough to mimic the time, it was a very weird sight, considering who we all were and where we were going.

Disembarking into what now was our first foray into the Sahara Desert, all that needed to be done was locate tent 80 and meet the remaining tent mates that were befriended through various platforms many months ago. Tent 80 ended up being in the middle row of the bivouac, which comprised 3 rows in the rough shape of a circle minus an eighth. These tents are black Berber-style tents made from goat hide, a heavy material where one could see the thick thread used to hold it together or patch holes. It was held up with a series of large and small sticks, which allowed access from both sides. Fastened down with pieces of rebar. I was the first man to find the tent and immediately chose a side as I like my back to a wall and felt at least I'd have a bit of comfort with a man only one side of me.

It was quite windy on that first evening, and straight away sand was getting everywhere, even though the initial site was not sandy per se. We had a significant sandstorm, which was much akin to being on a very windy beach in the middle of January in Enniscrone, except this particular surface held our tents. None were blown away thankfully, as it was a very good stress test. This area was very stony and rocky with lava-like rock features. Storms were familiar, but the content was not. The first evening was really just for arrivals, leaving the following day for gear checks. It gave time to make final decisions regarding kit and food. However, I had made all of mine already and what I had was essentially what I had, or more so, what I wanted to keep.

On the first day, part of the tradition is to herd all 1,085 competitors into a number shape, which represented the edition of that particular year's race. This happened to be the 37th year. Ticker tape was erected and we assumed positions to make up our unique year number. Years ago, I guess helicopters took the photos, but these days it is all about drones. The drone swooped up and down and side to side and got the image of over a thousand people making a 37. I had heard that they used to sweeten competitors with a can of coke to keep them happy in the herd, but there was none forthcoming this time.

We were all starving already before the race briefing started, which was where the eclectic Patrick Bauer first grabbed the mic along with his translator. I was apprehensive about him. With the experience of the last number of years from sign up to then. With all that happened with Covid and the performance of the company that we bought our entries from, I didn't really give him a chance. I had already decided that he and the organisation were ruthless and any leaping and hopping about to pop music was just all part of a show. The man likes to talk and what could have been a 20-minute briefing took about an hour. All things covered included what to do with your SOS beacon explained from a truck to a thousand people and how to poo in a bag, using a stone.

We finally filtered, starving for food, to dinner, which was provided along with breakfast and dinner on the following day before full self-sufficiency began on the Sunday morning.[1]

---

[1] https://www.theguardian.com/lifeandstyle/2021/oct/25/marathon-des-sables-runners-say-organisers-failed-in-duty-of-care

As the Marathon Des Sables was cancelled for me and others with COVID in 2020 and in 2021 the race was pushed out until a new date in October 2021. Having had two cancellations already, my opinion at the time was to push the race out to 2023.

At the time, I was still using Facebook and thus involved in several groups online to prepare for the race. What unfolded in the October edition 2021 of the Marathon Des Sables could only be described as some sort of war zone. Unfortunately, half the competitors failed to finish as many had contracted some sort of vomiting and diarrhoea bug in the camp, this coupled with unseasonably high temperatures (more on that later) where the gauge went up to 52 - 56 degrees, depending on what you read.

Heat stroke and a suspected stomach bug debilitated many people. Since then, I have heard stories of people who would cut pieces off their socks with a knife to use for the bathroom, such was the levels of sickness about the camp. The GPS trackers and medical staff were overwhelmed with many medical staff and support crews falling ill also, watching both as part of groups full of peers, reading reports in the media and hearing stories from competitors that had pulled out of the race seemed like a disaster from start to finish.

Personally, I was not too enthused about experiencing what those souls were going through in October 2021. I tried many attempts to get my investment in the race back as I wanted to pull out of the 2023 edition after all I had seen and heard. It looked like an absolute shit show as reported by the

Guardian and at that point, having invested a small fortune in the experience, I wanted to pull out and get as much hard-earned cash back.

Fortunately, my bluffs and from what I have heard since the bluffs of many an Irish man did not work, and with that Celtic stubbornness unbeknownst to each other it was decided that if I paid my money and can't get it back, I'm going to do the 2023 edition and by God I am going to enjoy it.

So, to say many were conscious of food provided was an understatement. Aaron was confident, and his confidence made me feel more confident whereas Ronan was not feeling well, so decided to hold off on what was provided and ate his own expedition foods.

It turned out there was no salad anyway, mostly everything was cooked. You could even have a Moroccan beer with your dinner if you liked. Sitting down eating at low tables on mats on the desert floor, we were already getting used to the discomfort of not having things like chairs. The last seat we had was the bus in and that would be it for the duration of the week. It was funny how something so basic would become so plush.

As we were going back to our tents, it was getting dark and the reality of the situation was really sinking in. I had never camped out properly outside of a couple of festivals such as the Electric Picnic in the sunny south of Ireland, which was more about getting fecked up, sleeping and repeating. This was far more civilised, but in harsher conditions. We were all pretty beat after the early flights and transfers, so Tent 80 set about getting sleeping bags and mattresses ready. The down bags were needed as it can drop to freezing in the desert at night, the mattress also providing some insulation. However, it was forecast to be fairly warm at night, so I did not pack a down jacket or fleece top. There was a little bit of envy when some started blowing up mattresses and pillows for extra comfort whereas I went as light as possible and forego any sort of comfort using a very full bag as a pillow and what's called a "flexmat" mattress underneath. This was a folding thin piece of spongy foam material, which I had cut to size. It was a tad cooler that first night and I was a little bit worried that I should have listened to Alma and brought the fleece top, but I had already removed it from my kit back home in Crossmolina.

My first night in the desert was not bad at all. The ground was very stony and hard underneath and as I tend to sleep on my side; I kept flipping from one hip to another as they got sore after a while. It was uncomfortable, but manageable. I think if I had a proper blow-up pillow, it may have been slightly easier to sleep. My back was sore about my lumbar with the hard ground. Lying on my back was actually more uncomfortable than on my sides with back pain. It starts to get a little bright and bluey about 4:30am in the desert. Tent 80 lads rustle one by one until all are awake and milling about. I needed to go to the bathroom. I did not want to use the poo bags, which meant placing a plastic bag over a seat in a poo chair, which was in a phone box style tent. One would put a small stone in the bag and then do the business by throwing the biodegradable bag in the poo bin which was located beside the phone box tent.

I like to go au natural so I just went for a walk off site and found a nice quiet spot for myself. I felt there was less chance of germs there than a communal tent and furthermore, it's a way nicer experience, anyway. Business done over a hill that rose above the bivouac and campsite for all the organisation - was some site. 4 x 4's, army trucks and personnel, helicopters with people everywhere. It was like a forward battalion getting ready to go over the hill and engage the enemy.

We made breakfast for the first time, which was done using what are called Esbit cooking tablets. Roughly the size of a small sweet it would heat water to a desired temperature to add to my breakfast, which was a Flahavan's porridge sachet. It was alright, obviously nicer with honey, but no comforts were added, so it was just downed along with some lukewarm water.

With the heat starting to pick up there was a moratorium on saying, "Jaysis it's hot, ha" or any variants of same. Heading for gear checks, everyone was already very conscious of staying hydrated and in the shade as much as possible.

Word was coming through that the organisation was just weighing bags and not individually checking equipment. There is a lot of compulsory equipment required to be self-sufficient for the week. One's food calorie count needs to be at least 14,000 calories and I had just over 18,000 made up of porridge, protein powder, expedition foods, vegan cous

cous dinners, tail wind in race nutrition sachets and cliff block jelly bars. You have to have a venom pump extractor, first aid, sleeping bag, compass, signalling mirror, sun cream and safety pins.

Outside of these I had a pair of compression tights for recovery, spare shorts, spoon, anti-bacterial gel, toothbrush and paste, 6 small packs of tissues, mug as a small stove, lighter, bottles which attached to my run bag, sudocrem, gurney goo, go pro, friars balsam, medication, and one spare pair of socks. And I kept the cotton t-shirt I was wearing. My run backpack came to 6.4 kg and my front run pouch was a little over 2 kgs, so total weight to start the first day was just shy of 8.5 kgs.

Now boiling, we wanted to time going up to get the checks done. Nobody wanted to stand around waiting to be checked in the mid-day sun but I was getting aggravated and just wanted rid of my second bag with civvy clothes for after the race. Tent 80 Jack and I went for it, getting rid of our second bag of clothes first before dealing with the gear check organisers and doctors.

I provided my ECG printout to the doctors and was asked about my family's health history regarding any heart issues to which I said there were none even though as an 8-year-old boy I called up to see my grandad Danny Hiney, went into his sitting room and sat up on his lap whilst he was having or just had a heart attack. I gave him a kiss and went on my way home, informing my mother that Papa's face was very red and blue. Funny the things you remember. There is no need to deliver this information to the male French doctor, I thought. They would have sent me for a second ECG or worse.

After withholding some information we had our SOS beacons attached to our run bags. These beacons were about the size of a cigarette box, they have several buttons on them that can be pressed in case of a medical emergency. They are also used to track competitors, both for race officials and those who are watching on from home. These tiny dots in the middle of a desert expanse become all that loved ones have of their family member or friend as they make their way through the course. After the beacon was zip tied on, we were given three litres of water, coupled with what was now on my back and on my person, the only possessions I would have for the next seven days.

We all lorded as much lunch and dinner into us as possible, as that would be the last properly cooked fresh food we would eat until the final day in the desert. Meeting people from other countries and meeting Mayo man Austin Mortimer racing under the New Zealand flag was gas.

I was not nervous, I just really wanted to run. I hate tapering, it always puts me in bad form. Going from running loads too little to less and having been pretty sick in the ten days prior to departure where I did not really exercise at all, I was really wound up.

On our second night, we had a really bad sandstorm. Frantically we ran around, getting stones to hold down the tent. Dropping sticks to take the sail-like nature of the tent away. Sandstorms are mad. They whip up everything into a frenzy and are quite strong. They can blind the sun and really disorientate you. They drive sand along the ground and underneath the tents. Everything gets destroyed. They come and go but can take bits of equipment such as gaiters for shoes to keep the sand out easily. So thereafter I would never leave gear lying about outside my bag in camp in case one came in quick when I was not in the tent.

Once the storm abated and we settled down to get ready for race day some of the lads had some shots of Jameson whiskey as there is a tradition of some sort of pre-race party. The French eat cheese for example. Some have sweets, etc. The Berbers lit a large bonfire in the middle of the bivouac and then began to drum and chant. There were only five of six of them, but it was quite powerful and really calming as I laid down to rest and sleep for race day.

20. Alma And The Kids At Home

Deep down, I believe in order to finish a race such as the Marathon Des Sables, one needs to have a selfish or ruthless streak. Going to the Sahara Desert, leaving Alma and three kids behind for twelve days is selfish. Furthermore, I did not want to bring my phone for two reasons, number one being added weight and number two being that I just wanted to be off the grid and to focus completely on what I was doing. Being totally wrapped up in my goals and the execution of those goals, in my opinion, can be the difference between finishing and not finishing. There are easier ways of blowing €6,000 - €10,000, if one honestly factors in all the costs associated with the completion of the Marathon Des Sables. If you want to be selfish blow it on a lads or girls holiday, buy a new car or what not.

However, behind my selfishness and ruthlessness was a family unit that was totally engrossed in what I was doing in one of the most inhospitable places on earth. Alma had all the Tent 80 crew and also all the other Irish competitors listed out on a piece of paper and was following each with my son Danny like it was the World cup. Using the GPS beacons to follow each of these competitors from different backgrounds, fly under an Irish flag. They took an interest in people I did not know, never mind them knowing the competitors. They would enter each of their finish times daily and monitor how they were progressing from start to finish for each Irish competitor. Being a crew member is a stressful experience, it is never a good idea to have a friend or family member crew a long Ultra Marathon. It is best to have someone with a bit of experience that knows what it all feels like and the mindsets that can develop within an athlete's mind. This time around, Alma and the kids were crewing from a phone and laptop in our family home in Crossmolina on the west coast of Ireland. A far cry from the scorched desert of the Sahara.

I can only imagine the stress my desires and goals put my family under. Not just for one day but for a multistage marathon, where a GPS signal could drop for a plethora of reasons, adding to the huge amount of stress that Alma would be already experiencing. The GPS beacons could go down for an individual athlete for thirty minutes to an hour.

This led Alma to be further stressed, which had a knock-on effect on Danny, who would also feel like something was not right. This all manifested with kids spending more time in Mammy's bed whilst Daddy was trying to prove something to himself.

I would love to tell you that this was something that was at the forefront of my mind throughout the twelve days away from home, nine days on the desert floor and six days racing. However, it was so far from my mind. I thought about my wife and kids regularly, but more so that they were there, rather than where they actually were mentally and spiritually.

Yet, these selfish and ruthless streaks, in my opinion, are as much a protective mechanism as much as what may be perceived as �win at all costs' mentality. Whilst others had their phones about the camp each evening, and if a signal allowed them to talk to loved one's outside the bubble, I think if I had done same, I would have been tipped over the edge. I needed that extra bit of hardness to keep myself resolute.

I could not physically walk to the internet tent for two evenings, when I could email home as I was quite emotional. This emotion is very hard to explain to those who do not undertake endurance type events that last for anything from ten to forty-eight hours. Imagine all the chemicals and hormones that one experiences in a game of football for sixty minutes, happening daily for ten hours. I see players do things that are out of character regularly because of the nature of emotion and sport during short periods. Over long periods, these emotions can just simply bubble over. Grown men and women will ball crying for little to no reason or on receipt of messages from home that were delivered daily to our tents.

To be focused on Alma and my three babies throughout such an experience and not parking them somewhat would make a tough experience even more impossible. For an amateur athlete, the ability to control, be selfish, be ruthless, to be an arsehole when needs arise is as much a safety mechanism and/ or a performance enhancer depending on the individual using these tools.

My eight-year-old boy, comforting his Mammy when the tracker would go down, makes me feel both sad for what I was doing but also proud how in tune my son was with his Mammy. When she was having a meltdown regarding a tracker, she missed talking to me, telling me about the daily goings on of life around Crossmolina and home. As soon as the kids were in school, she was straight home to the laptop focusing on pin size dots on a screen that had no discernible features such as rivers or trees, just an empty open expanse.

Daily, the kids would tick off a stage that Daddy just completed and send voice notes to my phone that was in a suitcase back at the hotel. They felt better that they had communicated to Daddy, and this was how they felt better about the process.

To understand me and my like and why I would do something like this under free will is to understand that I accept death. I am not afraid of being truly close to an edge whilst my children sleep soundly in their beds. As long as they are there soundly. To understand some of us, one needs to know we want to put ourselves in these situations as close to that line as possible, but know ourselves well enough that we are quite emotional creatures and need to protect ourselves from ourselves in these situations.

Maybe others do not think like this and I am an outlier or maybe it is Celtic fatalism but at certain points on that race in the highest heat of the day and over some of the most technical stretches I do not think that line was that far off.

Maybe one gets heat stroke, maybe one collapses, maybe they are found, maybe there is a pre-existing condition, maybe the Swiss cheese effect where all those Swiss cheese holes line up and an individual falls through the cracks on the sand.

Probably best that they did not know that, probably best that I stayed off the grid, probably best that I left my phone in my suitcase.

21 Sunday Day 1

21 Competitor drop outs

Finally, after nearly five years of waiting, the light illuminated the first bivouac. Once the blue glow came in, I nipped off to go to the bathroom and then come back and get ready. I liked to get dressed first. Getting all my kit on and fixing my gaiters. The gaiters attached to Velcro about the side midsole of the shoe and also attached at the shin. These plastic bags that looked like moon shoes prevent sand getting into your runners, which would cause blisters and general discomfort.

Once dressed, I made my breakfast and walked around eating it, trying to remain calm. After I had finished, I just lay back and meditated on my mat. I held my hand on my lower tummy and heart and tried my best not to think of anything and just focus on my breathing. My mam also meditates and we share an image to meditate on. I find this can be powerful and it chills me out, which was needed as the Berbers bring down the tents and we are exposed to the sun with no cover.

In Morocco, the clocks go back an hour for Ramadan. We had those arriving using Greenwich Mean Time and those arriving from the French charter flights using Central European Time. We were told that the clocks would go back but would revert to GMT for our desert time, but this was not the actual time. Everyone was going around switching the phone times to Iceland with their watches on another time and nobody seemed to know the actual fecking time.

First day was to start at 8:30am. We each saddled up. I had a run bag and front pouch with my mattress tied with my dad's golf bag bungee cord to the back of my bag. I drank the remaining water in the bottles they gave us the previous night and I was good to go.

As I have mentioned already, the race director Patrick Bauer likes to talk, with everyone just really amped to get going we were penned in and waited for the formalities such as which journalists were covering the race, top athletes present and other various bits of useless information that I had to interest listening to. Then we had the day's birthdays, which were called out whilst we listened to "Happy Birthday

To You " by Stevie Wonder, whilst Patrick Bauer and his translator, dad-danced on top of a white Land Rover Defender. Things got real when the charity runners and their buggy that contained a young boy were brought up to the front of the pack at the start line. And then finally the traditional AC/DC Highway to Hell began to play loudly as they gave us the countdown to go.

And finally, we were off running.

Tent 80 Alan was with me when the group started to spread a bit and settle. The ground was really stony. You have to be conscious of lifting your feet to avoid kicking large stones or tripping in general. The first few kilometres were a little bit of a drag uphill at about 6:00 min per km pace. I did not have my watch turned on yet so Alan was just checking if the pace was ok for me. I was saving my watch charge for later in the week.

Pretty much immediately, the heat became very apparent. My mattress was coming loose, so I had to carry it and I was feeling really out of sorts after several kilometres. I would have expected more of a stronger feeling of buzz or strength than heavy legs and general zappy vibes. We continued to our first jebel ascent. A jebel is a mountain, and they come in many shapes and sizes and degree variants. The first was, I know, now small, but at the time it seemed to unfold a massive lunar landscape both behind and in front of me.

As steps were chosen carefully, the sound of helicopters passing was pretty awesome as the media and medical crews worked and got ready to work. The stones and stoniness of it all were probably the first real big surprise about the terrain. These places have been seas at one point and many stones that you pass have fossils on them. Nearly as common as weeds in a field at home. Coming out of this former sea and into a wadi, we were greeted and cheered by local Moroccan boys of whom I thought, along with all we met within camps from Berbers to workers were super happy and friendly. What was not super happy was my already faltering performance. Already finding the effects of the heat quite debilitating, I wondered if I still had that virus flu thing from the week previously. I was not feeling on top of my game.

Then we hit the first dune field where I met and was passed by Brian from Kerry. We had a quick chat and we both talked about running on feel. Running on feel can only be described as ignoring what ones run watch and the environment is telling you and focusing on what is happening within your own body and mind, a watch may say that your heart rate is going through the roof but you may feel fine. Running on feel comes with experience where runners know they are not as bad or may not be as bad as can be suggested or, in this instance, a little bit wary or nervous about the day ahead, so we were both running on feel. Finally reaching our first CP (control point) or what we would know at home as a transition.

This is where the water situation really started. We could get 1 x 1.5 litre bottles of water here officially, which I grabbed and refilled my 2 x 750 ml run bag bottles that attach to the front of my bag. Complete with straws they are easy to use. I did not wait around for long and got on my way. With 13.2 kms done of the first stage, we had a shorter stage to 24.6kms at CP 2. But this is where I saw where the wheels were coming off for some athletes already.

Arriving at the second dune field, I had to walk. The heat was really getting to me. I saw a guy sitting down on a small clump of hard sand. It was like seeing the first person get shot. Sitting down maybe already overheating to me. It really was an early sign that something was not entirely right here. The heat in the dune field was something savage and for the first time I would see a glimmer of a CP far ahead that, like in a mirage from a desert movie, seemed close, but yet was so far away. Upon getting to this CP I took 2 bottles or 3 litres of water and sat down on the mat of a tent to get out of the heat. I was joined by many of my competitors, all trying to get heart rates down and cool off. This at 24kms on day one of a week's long excursion into a sandy unknown. I was already starting to feel very overwhelmed by what I was doing.

It took about 10 to 15 mins for me to get it back together again. I downed my water, filled by tailwind race nutrition bottle and added the sachet, filled a water bottle, drank the left-over water and headed off to complete the stage of 36 kms, of which 12 were left. What was a run, then a run walk, was now a walk.

People seemed to drop like flies, decent trees with cover became a magnet for people. First one or two, then maybe three or four under a tree. Even though I was not feeling like a champion, I thought well, at least, I'm not lying under a tree like a ghost. Eyes gaunt and skin pale. I kept marching on as well as I could. I tried to take my mind off things by chatting to a few people, including an American girl who informed me she was with her husband who was just a few metres up in front. I got the feeling she thought I was trying to chat her up, even though I was actually focused on survival. I hiked on past the odd looks of her husband. Whatever the feck a couple was doing this for together anyway, my wife finds me hard work going to the beach with the kids in hot weather. We would have killed each other doing this race. But each to their own, I suppose.

I guess many people have notions, notions with materialistic things or themselves. My actual notions revolve around my race times and performance, where I feel I should be versus the actual reality. As we began our ascent of Amessoui jebel whatever notions I had about how well I was or would not do in the 37th edition of the Marathon Des Sables were quickly dispelled. The sun was now blazing down on me and my performance hopes were quickly fading as we moved up a mountain one step at a time.

Prior to leaving for Morocco, I had told Alma that I should run about 10kms an hour on average. What planet was I on saying something like this? We will never know.

As the specific terrain was already doing its best to break anyone and everyone that was ascending, I was going well into the late 5 hour mark as I ascended this jebel with what was only a few kilometres to go.

The jebel was walkable but combined with the heat, it soon became a total grind. A gust of wind nearly took my hat with it. I was actually on edge. Upon ascent, they informed us that the bivouac was just around the corner. But just around the corner is different in the shimmer of heat and slow descent. Sand, rocks, sand, rocks, it was really hard to build any sort of rhythm with one eye on the first finish line. Trying my best to run fast in order to bring some sort of time performance into my stage result was stop start in nature to cross the line in my first stage at 6:08.

I was shocked to be honest. Shocked at what had just happened to me that day. Shocked at my performance after 5 years of preparation, I wondered what I was doing there and at. How crap I was at running considering the time and effort I put into it. Between training, strength and conditioning, yoga, nutrition, tee total life, bed for 10pm. What was the point of it all? To be there waiting on a Moroccan tea upon finishing. This hot, sweet liquid hits the spot. The sugary sweetness gives a little lift as we pick up our 6.5 litre water allocation to last us until the first CP of the next day.

Still in the heat I had to walk back to Tent 80 with now an added 6.5 litres of water in weight. It is only a few hundred metres, but it adds insult to injury. Getting to our abode, Alan, Ian, and Jack are already there and everyone looks absolutely messed up. Delirious even.

It becomes very apparent quickly that my thoughts and feelings about the day are not isolated. In fact, they are all on point. I manage to pull out my mattress and lay back down in my corner waiting for my heart rate to come down whilst I downed 1.5 litres of water like it's a mouthful. People start to trickle in and around the sight one by one and they all have the same look. A 4 x 4 land cruiser ambulance arrives to a tent further down. We later find out someone needed mouth to mouth resuscitation. It all seems too dramatic as the first day hits everyone like a sledgehammer. The individual survives and is fine. I somehow quickly put the news to the back of my mind. It is information that one mentally glances at but yet dismisses as quickly as possible in order to keep the semblance of a mentally stiff upper lip in such trying conditions.

The cut off for the 36k stage is 10 hours. Some of our Tent 80 boys cut it fine. On the first day, it already leaves very little leeway going forward. In comparison, if one had several hours to spare, you could allow time to recover, allow the heart rate to come down and eat. Those that were sailing close to cut off dropped their bags at the tent.

Those with feet problems dig out their medical cards and head to Doc Trotters for the first time at the medical tent to get blisters lanced, needles placed under toenails to drain the puss and have iodine injected into sores in order to disinfect and clean these areas of the feet. With the telltale signs of red markings on feet and legs like the war paint of an Apache Indian. These markings were not something that I was in any way jealous of. They indicated suffering.

That evening, I started to feel unwell. The lads were asking me if I was ok, and I was "Ya,100%". I guess I just went quiet. I could not talk. Only lie there. I was welded to my mat.

Understanding I needed food, I took a protein recovery post-race and then made my first vegan cous cous dinner. Still feeling unwell, I got up to pee for the first time that day. We were all checking the colour of our urine as an indication of where our bodies were at. Mine was middle of the road. Considering I had approximately 7.5 litres of water taken at this stage with salt tablets for each bottle, to have one pee was a bit concerning.

I started feeling nauseous, really confused why I was feeling this way. I hadn't eaten anything too off the wall and I had tested everything prior to coming to Morocco. Why was I feeling so sick? I got that tell-tale feeling that I was going to get sick, so I peeled myself off my mat and went around the side of the tent. Thankfully, it had started to get dark as there were lots of people milling around their tents. I could not get too far away from my tent, my body retched and then I started vomiting what seemed all the water I had ingested over the previous number of hours. I was actually mortified getting sick like this as, for some reason, it was like I was failing at the task at hand. I vomited a second time, just as bad as the first. More water projected from me, but thankfully, that seemed to be it as I made my way back into the corner of my tent space.

I was actually really embarrassed and felt bad vomiting about the tents having not made it out back a few metres away. Feeling very woozy, I went back to my corner. I could not really talk as I just lay there, incapacitated. Some lads moved about doing errands, coming back from the medical tent. We eventually settled down and got ready for bed. Day

1 was done. I was now apprehensive. Apprehensive for the next day as my belly gurgled and spluttered. Where might I go? I wondered if I would have to get up and get sick again? Slowly, I fell asleep but shoes and head torch were at the ready should I need to move fast out of my down sleeping bag.

22. Monday Day 2

31.7 km climbing 760 metres jebel tijekht, jebel otfal

106 Competitor drop outs

The second day began for me with diarrhoea. I essentially shat my brains out. There are several both obvious and not so obvious issues here. You start thinking many things such as, is this me for the day? And, if so, how much tissue will I use? What are the ramifications on tissue stock then for the week ahead? It's not the most humanly comfortable thing at the best of times, but imagine what it's like in a desert area with little to no cover and or privacy about a course! So, whilst rationing Kleenex and disinfecting my hands with anti-bacterial gel, I walked back to my tent.

I got dressed, got my gaiters on, then Hoka speedgoat runners and set about making breakfast. I had a cup of green tea and porridge. Once done, I lay back and meditated once more. I focused on my breathing with a hand on my lower tummy and a hand on my heart. The gurgling and spluttering had subsided as the time came to saddle up and move out. By now I was bungee cording the mattress to the top of my run bag. Treble knotting the darn thing as well as I could to prevent a repeat of the previous day's hassle. It waited like a satchel of straw on the top of my run bag.

We made it down towards the run start where it was a bit slower to gather. Patrick and his translator shadow were trying to cajole those still leaving their tents to hurry up. What should have happened was the shite talk to start instead of waiting for all to arrive and then start the shite talk. I was already a veteran of French shite talk converted into English shite talk, whilst two grown men danced on top of the famous Land Rover defender. The image of this vehicle has stood the test of time throughout this desert and deserts, it may be starting to get phased out with larger and more comfortable vehicles such as the modern-day Toyota Landcruiser. For 37 years in this race the land rover defender has been a stable be that for ferrying sick or injured and or dad dancing on top of its roof.

Once everyone finally arrived, we got some information. Most of it useless for the day ahead bar "take your salt tablets". We got the leader board run down and more ominously heard there had already been some 21 dropouts on day one. It was like receiving the death notices on Mid West Radio before radio bingo, where our regional radio station in Co. Mayo to the delight of my grandparents back in the day would listen to the deaths about the county being read out daily through a drawl respectful voice. It was always somewhat disappointing for them if they did not know any names that were mentioned, this disappointment only however short-lived when the radio bingo would take place directly after, the Yin and Yang of their morning life whilst getting ready for their 10 am dinner.

But no time now to give too much thought about all that preparation and a small fortune paid for those to have to medically pull out after day one. "Highway to Hell" blared out as we all headed off once more. The plan for me - run like hell to get out of this heat as quickly as possible. We had started earlier, so should be out of the afternoon raging inferno a bit earlier. I was going to run where I could and hike where I had to.

Moving nicely with my tummy abated, the river of runners minus a few comrades snaked its way toward the first CP at 12.6 kms. Soon, every now and again, runners started to peel off and drop their shorts. For all the talk about solidarity with the Marathon Des Sables, this is where I felt some of the actual solidarity was, you gave them space to go to the toilet there and then, mere metres from passing runners. That space was ignoring the person who was in your peripheral vision trying to get through a day's stage with gastrointestinal issues. Thankfully, I was feeling fine as I sipped on either water or my tailwind nutrition every 10 minutes. I tried eating some of the cliff block cubes. Having brought a large box of them, I was surprised at how few I had eaten the previous day.

I kept running as much as possible with the jebel Hered Asfer starting to come into view. Helicopters circling, Tent 80 Jack passed me out with his super-fast march hike even though I felt I was running as quick as I could. Such is the power of a good hike run approach. Even that early in the morning, my heart rate was starting to climb. Combined with the ascent, I was really struggling and started getting passed out. It was a walk climb rather than a slow climb, but it was quite tough. I would try to focus on short distances rather than look at the entire ascent. Just focusing on small bites as I made my way to the top and scooted along the ridge line where my body now recovered as I observed all those amazing rocks, each with their own brief story. With 4 odd kilometres to go to CP one I was managing my hydration and nutrition well and nearly forgotten about my tummy at that stage.

We were being given two bottles of water now at the CPs. I think the realisation of the heat wave and its effects were really starting to hit home. Maybe the previous 1 bottle policy at certain CPs in the printed handbook showed that the organisation did not realise themselves how hot this later than normal edition would actually go down with

Ramadan later this year. The race itself starting the day after Eid Mubarak.

I had a process now; grab bottles, find a free spot in a tent, lie back with my bag still on to rest my shoulders. Down a 1.5 litre of water. Get a tailwind sachet out and refill the nutrition bottle, fill the other bottle with water and drink the remainder, or pour it over my head. Trying to keep all of this to 10 minutes, I laboured up and got going again.

There were 12 kilometres to the next CP which included the Joua Baba Ali jebel. On the way I asked a French guy how many kilometres we had to go. I quickly realised once he answered that he was deaf. There was a group of deaf runners as part of this year's competitors. Not only could he understand what I said, he repeated the kilometre reading in French and with his hands. Leaving a nice hard compressed stony ground for sand and an ascent again affected my body greatly. Happy to have at least ran as much as possible, the 15% climb really took it out of me. One step at a time trying to leg press a leg up, then the next whilst those in front may slip and slide and or take timeout for a rest.

Taking a minute rest would allow the heart rate to come down slightly as we tried to navigate what was a formidable vertical climb that got steeper and steeper and seemed to knock the absolute stuffing out of me. I was using poles which helped displace weight and I could use my upper body more. Having not used the poles on the first day, the weight of my bag and stress of being hunched over in the heat killed my shoulders. My shoulders felt like there were two golf balls stuck about where the straps were. I stuffed my spare

Star Wars cotton t-shirt in between my shoulders and the straps to alleviate some of the discomfort. At least more upright, even when climbing, it helped the shoulder pain also and the better posture aided in creating a more stress-free posterior chain.

Having ascended and crested the ridge line, the body quickly adapts and begins to relax again somewhat. The rocks and shale became sandy once more as we dropped onto the flats. I tried to pick up the pace again but it was like running in an oven. With my hat pulled right down trying my best to minimise the abuse of the sun grinding down the 4 odd kilometres was like a sick joke with being able to see the CP way off in the distance. Competitors would pass you running then burn out and start walking. I would build up the revs and pass he or she out for a few hundred metres and then also gas out. This cat and mouse game was common. A person's run feel was dictated by the oven they were in along these ancient flats that were once the bottom of the sea. The mirage of a hill in the distance never seemed to get any closer no matter how much impetus was injected. Grinding slowly, surely, and consistently hoping that the water in my bottles would last. As Tent 80 scuba guy Ian would attest, there were striking similarities between being here running out of water compared to being under the sea and running out of air. Pulling dry on your bottles with a few kilometres to go would send a shiver down your spine in what we know now was toward or just above 52 degrees of heat.

Reaching the CP before the final jebel of the day, El Otfal, there was no point in any sort of rush as the gradient here was 25%. And you could see every part of that gradient staring down at you with a very evil sandy stare. Our Tent 80 Rebel renamed this jebel, "Jebel go fuck yourself" for a very good reason. This huge gradient hulked over the CP like a massive, indifferent monster waiting to be challenged. One could not even see any ant-like human shapes, such was the height from afar.

The climb was criminal. It had to be broken down psychologically into stages or else one would have made the dreaded Y shape with your arms in order to be collected and brought back to the bivouac in a helicopter. The initial previous climb was rocky, so one could grip. This started off essentially as one great dune that just went vertical. I was putting force into both legs and arms via poles just to keep moving. Those above looked like insects such was the size of the jebel.

There was just no respite. Unrelenting climbing that dog legged dune to reach rocks that even though they provided greater foot stability, the action of standing and moving so vertically absolutely nailed me. I had to take several breaks and sit down on hot rocks that burned the arse off me. It was a slow grinding caravan that made its way vertically at one point, having to climb what I could only describe as a hot Hillary step. The cold Hillary step being the last hard piece of climbing that climbers face as they summit Mount Everest in order for competitors to reach a rope to aid them to complete the last section of the now once sandier vertical climb. It was fecking horrific. With several people now holding a climbing rope marshalled by a few, what seemed like media crew, as now we had to contend with rope burn. One guy put the rope between his legs and nearly had a cheap job done for the ‘snip’. I guess the climbing 101 book states never put the rope, between your legs in these situations.

Even looking how the rope was drilled and screwed into the wall seemed intense. The nut and bolt looked so out of place against a black rock at the top of a jebel in the middle of a desert. But then what was normal about it all?

I summited and sat down on a hot rock cooking like a fried egg. Got my head in gear and started to descend the jebel along what was like a rock river. With black river-like rock surrounded on both sides by brown rock, there was no fast descent. It was one step at a time. Trying to find one's feet with poles getting caught between the rock veins. The poles getting stuck required a quick jab like removal, 3 limbs moved whilst one was stuck in position. It became very frustrating navigating this ancient rock river. The descent even seemed to go on forever, the heat aided with preheated rocks for added extra absolute carnage.

Making our way out of the mountain range, we entered a dune field and whilst only just over a kilometre long they absolutely sucked any remaining life out of me. This whilst being able to see the finish line that never seemed to get any closer, no matter how much I ran or hiked. Just a wavy shimmer in the distance.

Finishing what was a shorter stage of 31.7kms in 6 hours :37 mins was insane. The jebels had a massive toll and after a cup of well-earned Moroccan tea and grabbing my 6.5 litre water allocation until the first CP of the next day; I made my way back to Tent 80 where Alan, Ian and Jack were waiting. They looked just as deranged as I felt, and it was quite obvious that things were not going well for almost everyone.

Collapsing onto the Moroccan rug that made up our tent floor, I had difficulty getting my mattress out. My heart was still pumping and taking an age to calm down as I took my gaiters and shoes off to allow my feet to breathe and the swelling go down. We were all talking to each other but not talking if that makes sense. Eyes were just piercing into the distance as to what had happened that day.

The lads all filtered back 1 by 1 with two of our group leaving the time very fine once more. They were quite relaxed about it. Dropping bags and going to Doc Trotters to get blisters lanced, cut, injected and Indian branded.

I was glued to my mattress for the evening. The lads asking me if I was ok. "Ya 100%", I would say. Although I just could not really talk, only moving to go to the toilet. There is an Internet tent on site that one can send one email at a time through their system. I was conscious of sending Alma and the kids an email as we were getting delivered emails from people at home to our tent, which was very emotional for everyone, especially with the condition that we were in. Many just simply welled up when they read an email note from a family member, friend or, in some cases, complete strangers. It had a massive uplifting effect.

There was not a hope I could summon the energy that evening to walk the 300 odd metres to type a few words home. I was in a hoop, but the delivered messages made me very emotional and gave me a great lift - especially from my kids, who wondered if I had seen a scorpion yet or how sandy it was.

23. Tuesday Day 3

34.4k jebel El Otfal , jebel Zireg

72 competitor drop out

Like any community, there is an element of community gossip. It's a very porous organisation with so many people involved from media, medical, Berbers, general organisation operatives, drivers and everyone else. Also at this stage most of the lads in Tent 80 had visited the Doc Trotters (medical tent). Obviously, with our neighbour tent mates from the UK and Netherlands in front, we were privy to all the stories starting to move around our little world in the middle of one of the most inhospitable places on earth.

It was quite obvious there was absolute carnage on the course. Rumours of further dropout rates were quite high. Having since had 106 dropouts confirmed for day two. We joked the helicopter pilots had the famous Credence Clearwater Revival anti-Vietnam song, "Fortunate Son" on repeat such was the manner of Hueyesqe Vietnam- era movements to and from the camps as there were people being pulled off the course or having medical misadventures.

There was a very slow walk to the start line on the third day. However, I was personally very conscious of the fact that my placings had dropped from the high 200's to the high 300's after the second stage so I really wanted to put a good shift in on day 3. I was not feeling sick anymore and my GI system seemed to have settled greatly. The day 3 stage suited me a lot better with a bit more areas to run.

But before we got going we had to endure the formalities. At this stage, I felt anyone that had a birthday should have been taken out and shot. I don't know if the organisation have a list or did they put their name forwards because the sound of "happy birthday to you" blaring out was actually starting to tip me over the edge. This after revealing that there were approximately another 106 dropouts the previous day, to an audible groan from the crowd in front. At least with the issues with heat we were now starting an hour earlier at 7am rather than 8am. But the extra bit of shite talk and translated shite talk meant a 7:05 – 7:10 start invariably.

Cue "Highway to Hell" and we were off and I actually felt good and ran what was a bit of a drag with the river of now very smelly competitors. So smelly nobody noticed anymore. Making our way onto what I could describe as mountain bike single track I really got in the groove. We were flanked by really cool dune buggies. These things seem to be mainly made out of suspension as they zipped up, down and around, sometimes with music blaring and a doctor dancing. Which, funnily enough, helped greatly.

One needed to be focused on each step, if you kicked a stone. You may kick the same bloody stone 3 times or simply fall and if you fell on these stones you would be shredded. Some competitors started to peel off once more and deal with their diarrhoea. You just ignored the poor devil who was trying to hold onto some form of decency and privacy by squatting behind an imaginary cover, because there was none. But it was quite obvious that many were suffering the same type of GI distress which may have been brought on by the extreme temperatures with digestive systems unable to deal with these combinations.

Even that early, the oven was getting hard to run in, but I was super focused that morning to get as much of the course run as possible and minimise walking to improve my standing and simply get out of the heat of the day. With an hour earlier start and any time improvement, I felt I could get into cover for a larger portion of the day compared to the previous days.

The single track opened up onto what I could describe as a dried-out lake with a previous mud bottom. It felt hard but hollow, like you could punch through into another world. It was nice to run on and gave a nice piece of security. I caught up with Tent 80 Alan, who was way ahead of me the two previous days, so that gave me a great confidence boost that I was pacing well that morning.

Soon we saw our first scorpion, a little black thing. It was the only live beast I had seen bar the dog someone from the organisation had in the camp. Some English guy had a GoPro stuck in the scorpion's face as I ran past them both.

Soon the pace began to slow with more sandy sections. For the most part I had ran most of the two CP's and felt I was doing a lot better but still being cautious taking my time in the CP's getting as much water in as possible and taking time in the shade especially. These few minutes were so important to drop the body's core temperature. My heart rate would drop 30/40 beats in a few minutes and once exiting the CP greatly rehydrated and with a lower core temp and heart rate, I felt a little bounce.

Just as well, because the next section to finish the day was horrific.

On the way I met Brian from Kerry again which was nice because the brief chat broke up the section a bit. It was very sandy, hilly and full of dunes so we were hiking it. I of course, guaranteed him that this was Mayo's year and we were 100% going to win the All-Ireland.

It was good to talk but it actually takes a lot of energy to talk and walk in that heat. Brian's pace was slightly faster, so he just pulled away and I guess we both were happy to save all the energy we could. That or else he has a heap of money on Kerry to win Sam and I was wrecking his head! This of course similar to the story of the Boston Red Sox where annually a Gaelic Football mad county wonders if its search for a coveted All- Ireland Gaelic Football trophy the Sam Maguire cup will finally be won for a 4th time after a 73-year famine. I do genuinely believe that this year is our year with the quality of the panel irrespective of our own Babe Ruth style curse.

As we crested a rocky single-track path, what was ahead of us could only be described as a sea of dunes that resembled waves. These waves were about thirty feet high however instead of rolling towards us like the sea water would. They remained static, with each wave of sand requiring a huge amount of energy to climb on step at a time whilst the sand would move and slide and suck you into the dune. If we were surfing, we could have it out back into a calmer ocean in order to catch our breath, however here there was no such place to let a heart rate come down and allow me to catch my breath. This was the Marathon Des Sables, the toughest foot race on earth. There was no place to rest, there was only the sight of another huge jebel up ahead of us.

I could not see any ant-like humans walking on the mountain. I was hoping that maybe we did not have to climb what was in front of us and we could hook left to what looked like a wadi or riverbed. They would not do that to us before the long stage, I mused. The level of technical strain delivered by the organisation was too tough for the heatwave that met it that was now enveloping most of Spain and north Africa, apparently.

One foot over the other as I trudged forward, seeing the ants now, seeing the body shapes snake up a ridge. Feck it. I can't believe we have to climb this. This is sick, I thought. Cold, ruthless, horrendous.

One foot over the other. I compartmentalised what was in front of me. Picking a dog leg and just focusing on that, a rock, a bush, a clump of sand. Whatever–don't look at the summit just what is 50 odd metres in front of me.

The heat was now becoming unbearable as I put the strain into my climbing poles, sometimes hanging onto those poles stuck in the sand for dear life just to get some rest. Just stop, take a moment. As my 4 limbs moved in unison, I repeated a Dr Joe Dispenza walking meditation introduced to me by my "head Coach" a Dr Joe Dispenza affiliate Mairead Gordon. 2-4-6-8, 2-4-6-8, 2-4-6-8, repeating it over and over, trying my best to take my mind away from the strain on my body.

Upon reaching Dog Rock, I looked up at the sandy dune that hugged this mountain and picked the next line. Trudging forward, I actually thought about Mount Everest and how hard it must be to climb. With my heart in the red zone and the heat now well into the high 40s or greater, I thought I could actually die here. I thought that this was what the death zone must be like. Being in such a precarious place that there is no up or down, no over or back, just where you stand and your body's own reaction to this position it finds itself in. I think right there was the closest I had ever come to feeling my mortality as a human. I have never felt such a foreboding sense of my infallibility.

One foot in front of the other. Don't stop. 2-4-6-8 I dog-legged up to come back down slightly, which offered the tiniest bit of respite once more, before coming onto a more stable rock single path surface that was easier to walk on even though higher than the previous section. Scaling that peak and checking out the bowl valley behind offered no solace, only to crest once more into a sandy descent to which many were saying the same thing.

Where the feck is the finish line? With 4 kilometres to go into what I thought was a great expanse it should be revealing itself by now. With each corner, it stays hidden. Way ahead I see a green wadi with what looks like some form of tents. It can't be that far for 4 kilometres. I was really starting to crack up until finally I hear an American whoop with delight "There it is", dropping below the banners and insignia which were so well tucked that gave a sense of closeness. And ending.

I was starting to feel better looking at the expanse of the bivouac with its black circles of tents. Feeling that I was actually going to make it through the week. Confident now that I would finish the challenge with day 3 nearly complete.

Arriving in at 5:57 those 3 minutes makes me feel a whole lot better about my performance and ability. It gave me such a boost that I was smiling. I felt I went out to do a job on the stage and I got it done. Timely, before the long day.

With day 3 done and dusted, after our early morning lecture that we were getting enough water- they gave us extra water that evening. I think the level of dropouts at that point led the medical officer to make and or force a decision here. It was only that morning that we were essentially told, "Ye have enough water". This is the Marathon Des Sables. To be then told later that evening we were getting an extra bottle was the usual Marathon Des Sables goalposts shifting. I was not complaining. After a stage by the time I rehydrated, cooked, rehydrated and drank more electrolytes, cooked breakfast and filled my run bottles there was very little left out of 6.5 litres. The extra 1.5 litres made such a difference. Even though these bottles we were receiving were essentially lukewarm to hot, if you added a tea bag into the bottle, you could have had a half decent cup of tea. And that is a regret, that I did not bring a box of teabags to put into the water as it would have made such a difference ingesting lukewarm to hot bottled water. This was also starting to have some sort of effect on my body and GI system. Towards the end of day 3, I was retching my in-race nutrition tailwind. I knew deep down that this was a problem.

That evening, I had a little bit more energy and after several threatening yet uplifting messages from my wife and kids about my lack of contact I made my way to the Internet tent to send an email to them. It was the first time I felt somewhat human since we started the previous Sunday. I was not buzzing for day 4, the long stage of 90 kilometres. But I was certainly ready.

24. Wednesday Day 4

The long stage 90 kms Jebel Zireg Jdaid 36 hour cut off into rest day

119 competitor drop outs

I am not afraid of distance. I have completed and attempted some absolute dogs of races. I have run 70kms, 77kms, and 100kms along with plenty of 64kms races. I had trained for 5 years in preparation for this race after all the comings and goings with Covid. This on the back of 7 Ironmans over as many years. Stephen Donnelly, my run coach, put me through a comprehensive run block in final preparation for this race. I do two strength and conditioning sessions per week with my coach, Darren Siggins, and I do at least two yoga sessions per week.

With all that preparation, I still felt I had come up short. Not because I was lacking in any form of coaching, but it was the event that lent itself to giving me that feeling that I was still missing something. But what, I do not know. It was a gut feeling, a rumbling gut and I was really nervous about that 90km long day.

It was the knowing. Knowing what was ahead of us. We were strategising in Tent 80. Ian, our chief strategist, was imploring to get to CP 3 and wait there for the heat to pass. Those that know me, know that I just run. I rarely plan ahead on a race, I either have a pace that I try and stick to or I go on feel. Sitting there listening to Ian knowing that he was 100% right, I was both disappointed at having to tow the company line but at the same time glad to have such cool, intelligent wise heads in the tent. They were leaders, strategists and very wise. I was blessed with luck to have their presence of mind.

The mix was great and so important. To have such successful people in the tent of all ages and backgrounds really made a team effort out of Marathon Des Sables. Nobody was stuck for anything be that toilet paper, batteries, food, creams, medicine, or an arm around the shoulder. With only a few days in, we had made a great bond with each other. Head to toe in the tent for comfort of sleep and head-to-head where needs be, we were there for each other. Doing what Irish men do for each other. Showing love, by giving each other dog's abuse.

Be that Jack and his raid- light hot pants shorts which were a crime to humanity or Johnny religiously taking everything out of his bag every night, looking at it and putting it back in the bag. Everyone, including myself, had their ‘isms’.

But we did really need each other that day. It was the making or breaking of the 37th edition of the Marathon Des Sables and I think everyone knew that deep down.

We started an hour earlier than the road book suggested once more that morning.

It was quite a dark start being waved on by the next batch of dropouts who were at the start line to see us off. They stood just off the race start line, kindly waving us on. It was big of them. I don't think I would have been as positive as they were. They showed great character, especially at the moment. There was no running for this start, as it was straight into sand. And with elevation. It was a slow drag for our long day. A conversational hike up and over. The top 50 runners started an hour behind us. This is normally a great opportunity to see the best runners up close as they pass.

It was an incredibly slow start to the long day with the climbs, dunes and sand so there was no headway to be made by running to at least put as many kilometres behind you as possible before the proper heat of the day started. Psychologically, if you had a good 30/40 kilometres done before the suffering started I feel it stands you in good stead.

But that was not to be. Only a ruthless cold organisation could survive in this heat. That initial slow start and drags set up for a horrendous stage. It took hours of walking to get anywhere. I could only run such a tiny amount. Arriving at CP's full of people already trying to get out of the sun at 8 and 9 am was very disconcerting.

I had opted to have a bottle of water and a bottle of electrolytes early on, as I felt it was going to be a long day with my race nutrition. As it had already made me retch the previous day. I was retching my porridge that morning so deep down I knew something was amiss.

After CP 1 I felt I'd better get some sort of nutrition into me so I tried to eat some cliff block jelly's. They came back up as soon as they went down. I was retching and vomiting. Even putting a jelly in my mouth made my body spasm and retch. I continued drinking my water and electrolytes and hoped things may improve over the day.

I have done ultra marathons where I may have walked for a few percent of the race, this may increase because of the severity of the race or the condition I may find myself in. In The Kerry way night run I ended up walking the final 18 kms of a 100 kms race as I was goosed, some ultras I have ran the entirety of the race. It is all race dependent, and athlete dependent. A good walk or hike strategy is as beneficial as running, as I soon found out. Some athletes are very strong hikers and can fairly move, such as our tent mate, Jack. I personally just prefer to run and do so when I can. However, and unfortunately, the long day of the Marathon Des Sables was a day for walking.

Coming into the flats where the heat was now in the high 40s, a mother and daughter came up to us with their billy goat. I think they were trying to sell some sort of nick-knack. If they were selling cans of coke they would have made a killing. So I just said "Salem" and politely declined, as we passed their herd of camels. Headed through a rock valley that looked like images of Moses holding the seas apart.

Passing the valley of El Maharch conservation of liquid was very important. I would take a sip every 10 minutes. Even though we had passed and were now in a very runnable section it was just impossible. The heat was in the low 50s. It was insane. As I reached CP 2 as passed by the race leader at the time Rachid El Morabity. He just glided past holding onto a bottle of water like he was doing a local park run.

Coming into CP 2 there was a tent that had a word that was written in French but looked like the word "Abandonments". It was full and sent another shiver down my spine. At this stage, Tent 80 had reconvened. Alan, Jack, Seamus, Ian and I were all now together again as we headed for El Otfal jebel or "jebel go fuck yourself" as we called it now. The next CP, CP 3 was where we all had intended to take a break.

The journey to this mountain started flat before it entered a dune field filled with squatters of a different kind. Once out of the dunes, the climbing started.

There was a man lying in the shade of a 4 x 4 Landcruiser. He did not look very healthy. This was the point, right there, with that man supported by a tyre wheel that things started to get very fecked up.

Having had issues with his nutrition, Alan, was now operating on fumes, deep down I knew what was happening, I knew that there was nothing that could be done, so I just ignored him and his issues as it was simply too hot to care about another person. Here in this environment any one thing will be found out and you will be beaten with it, in this instance Alan really suffered. It was the hardest part of the course that day and I believe possibly for the entire week, this is where he was at his lowest ebb. This is where he needed help, whether that help would have made any difference at that stage is unlikely, but looking back at a man's lowest ebb I cruised past not giving a fuck. If you can do the same, well, then the Marathon Des Sables is for you. If you are the type to go into a nursing mode, well, then I have some bad news. You may also end up on that scrap heap, your kindness may make you feel better, may make you feel like you are doing something good and you may be even ok, but right there, right then on the 1,500 metre ascent of the back side of jebel El Otfal you could end up most certainly similarly fucked up.

It was that hot as we began to ascend the jebel that I kept getting out of breath like I was unfit at the start off a GAA season back in the day. Bent over burst. We had already done this jebel previously from the other side so we knew what to expect. But this time it was different. It was way hotter.

So hot we had to sporadically stop every few minutes and catch our breath and allow the heart rate to come down. We entered what I can only describe as a gulley. A rock gulley that was preheated all morning. The heat came from the bottom and from the top now. And there was no escape. It felt like an oven with underfloor heating.

As we rounded a corner, we found other competitors that had secured real estate on the mountain that had about 15 metres long of shade. Without question, we all made our way over and shared the shade. It was beautiful. I hung my head in what looked like shame over my poles. Sucking in the benefit of that shade. Allowing the shade to mind me, hold me. Care for me. That shade was life. It was a booster. But soon we had to leave as we could not wait there forever.

Seamus trudged ahead first as I took extra rests. Burning my arse a few times on the hot rocks. I actually thought I gave myself a proper burn at one stage on my butt cheeks. Once more, it was one step at a time, so slow, so definite. I went to sit once more and fell over. The rock was at a slight angle and I was like a drunk trying to sit down on a park bench. I could not handle the slight change that a spirit level would have picked up on. I dropped my climbing poles. It was like I was losing control of my body trying to ascend this bastard of a jebel. Rounding corners and not seeing the summit wears down on you. Everyone is suffering, everyone has that look of sheer despair. Just wanting this mountain over. Blake, an American top 50 runner, passes me. I wish him well, he just turns around to me and with piercing blue eyes says "This is a bitch man".

Blake, a Texan, certainly not unused to these type of conditions–his 1,000-yard stare spoke volumes.

Finally summiting with Ian and Jack, we all collapse onto hot rocks. Where the CP had been the previous time when we came at this mountain from a different direction was not in the same place. This affected everyone's mental wellbeing. There were water consequences. Some took penalty bottles of water. This is where if you took a bottle of water at the top of the mountain, you were given a 30-minute time penalty. This was radioed by the guy with the water back down to the CP.

I was fecked if I was going to take a half hour penalty. I'd sooner suffer than give in to them. After a 12% climb in 50 degrees heat, we still had a 4-kilometre distance to cover before the next CP. This included the 20% descent with rope onto the dune of death.

It all just added into the delirium we were experiencing. We saddle up once more and make our way to CP 3, supposedly our saviour. Our paradise, what was to rekindle our ability to reach greatness? All roads led to CP 3 and rest.

Struggling to maintain water conservation, I just sipped as well as I could on what remained of my water and electrolyte drink. I still could not take in any race nutrition, be that tailwind or cliff block jellies. I was headed toward 36 kms with no in race nutrition on board. Somehow, I was managing.

Arriving at that CP was like a war zone. There was a lady with her back to a stand. Her legs were completely limp and white and she had the most red coloured face I have ever seen on a white person. It was like she had painted her face. It was insane. Her face looked like it was on fire.

I grabbed my water and found a corner. Lying back on my running backpack, I unclipped the buckle to allow myself to be more comfortable but upright. I was so tired that I started counting breaths 1,2,3,4,5,6,7,8,9,10 and repeat. I did this over and over again . I looked to my left and there was a Spanish man with his eyes open but it was like there was nobody home. His pupils were really small and he did not even notice me staring directly at him. People were just coming in and collapsing. It was fecking carnage.

I closed my eyes and tried to sleep. I could feel myself drifting. Hearing all the sounds and all the talking but drifting. Drifting away, but not to anywhere. Just trying to sleep. Just trying to rest.

As I laid there semi-conscious, I could get the smell a smell of a cigar or pipe. It was such an unusual smell. Why was there such a smell here? Why is someone smoking? Who is smoking? It was a nice smell. It was different smelling that smoke as I lay there. Still with my eyes closed smelling this inappropriate smell, I touched my nose. My nostrils were flaring, but I was not in control of my nostrils. They were flaring automatically. Why, I thought, are my nostrils flaring like that? They felt near muscular, my nostrils felt strong. But why were they flaring like that? Why were my nostrils doing their own thing? I opened my eyes. There is just delirium about. I ask Ian about the others. He said he didn't even know I was there, even though I was talking to him previously. We were all over the shop.

I closed my eyes. I think I slept, but I was conscious. Water was becoming an issue. If I started drinking from my bottles now I would reduce what I had to get me from the CP I was holed up in to the next CP. CP 4.

I told Ian about my predicament. I said, "I'm going, tell the lads." He had to get his blisters looked at by the doctors. Absolute dog suffering. I saddle up and get going. Get to 48.7 kilometres. Thankfully, the hour rest and time out of the sun helped. It was slightly cooler. Maybe the high 30s or low 40s but certainly not as hot as previously experienced ascending the jebel.

As I made my way, I met a nurse. I explain I keep getting sick and cannot keep my race nutrition down. She asks a few questions such as delirium and GI distress, but it's just vomiting, thankfully. Not mentioning anything about what I was experiencing in the previous CP. She gives me a tablet. I had motilium in my first aid kit as prescribed by my doctor, James, and dispensed by Strand Fitness member Martin both of whom saved my race with some great prescriptions for such an inhospitable location. However, one's brain does not work in these situations. I took the tablet, and she gave me a second to take later, explaining only to eat tiny amounts.

I thanked her and was on my way, looking over my shoulder as I walked, checking out the sun, willing it to go down and give us some respite. A break, anything, just a little time out. Marching as well as I could towards the CP I was actually moving well again. Promising a break for myself and maybe a cup of green tea.

Upon arriving to CP 4, life was starting to slow down greatly with the dropping sun. As I continually checked her progress by looking over my shoulder. As the sun dropped and those ahead snapped their glow sticks and turn on torches, I thought I'd leave all of that until I sat down. Taking off my bag now and searching for kit seemed like too much work.

Arriving at CP 4, people were lying about, some sleeping, some cooking. Some with vacant looks in their eyes. I took some time out, lighting up Esbits and making a cup of tea. I felt I deserved it getting past the halfway point and getting ready for the night stage of the race. I felt the little bit of caffeine in the green tea would help and it was going to be nice to have something that tasted different.

Taking maybe 20 minutes in total to sort my water drink, 1.5 litres, get the tea going and drink it, I saddled up once more and moved out. I'd say I got about 300 metres when I puked every bit of liquid I had just ingested up to and including that green tea up in the sand. I was nearly laughing. It was that pathetic.

Now, my body's tolerance to hold down water was faltering. An English guy behind me said, "That's the water mate. That happened to me too". It put me between a rock and a hard place. I could not eat. I had to hydrate but could not keep down water. My tummy did not seem to grumble as badly when I drank my lemon electrolyte mix, so I doubled the tablets and now had two electrolyte bottles. This is on top of already taking a salt tablet every hour. At least then I didn't experience the whole-body retch spasm that comes from deep down and makes you look like a cat that is trying to fire a fur ball out of its mouth.

The electrolyte mix seemed to work, as I now was in the dark with a longish stage of 13 kilometres to navigate. I was moving, but getting exhausted and sleepy. Eyes were droopy and my brain function slowing down to a trickle. However, still I was catching up to and passing those in front of me, which aided the sensation of moving towards the destination of finishing that bit quicker, but my body felt like a country that was running out of resources. I promised myself a nap at the next CP as a reward.

Arriving at CP 5 was like coming into the Electric Picnic afterparty in the wee hours of the morning. It was really quiet. People were resting, but some were now sleeping. This gave off the impression that "Oh, its ok to sleep". Sure, if they're sleeping, I can sleep. It certainly gave one carte blanche to be able to go to la la land. I grabbed my bottles unbuckled, collapsed and lay back on the tent.

Others who had the same idea quickly joined and flanked me. One pretty much touching up against me which in normal circumstances would mean that both parties would pull away from each other with the touch yet both parties were so fecking tired we just lay there!

I closed my eyes and felt myself starting to drift. It was like lying back in a warm bath. I could feel the pain and tiredness just start to melt away from my body. Seeping away all those feelings of discomfort. Draining down the plug and away from my being. It was so quiet and relaxed. I thought about completing the race later. Nobody cares, I thought. Nobody cares that you kept going or that you just had a little sleep. What do I have to prove to anyone? Nobody cares. Just enjoy the snooze.

And I did enjoy it until, on my left-hand side of my brain towards the back of my skull, a little voice said to me.

"Barry, get the feck up!"

I heard the voice. I acknowledged its presence. I wondered why it was coming from that side of my head when it again said.

"Barry, get the feck up!"

I was right, ok. Relax for feck sake, I'm getting up.

And I did, after about 20 mins some part of my subconscious or higher version of me told me to wake up and get going again and I did just that as my sleep buddies either side of me were now snoring.

I buckled up and saddled up and left CP 5 at the 63.3km mark and made my way to CP 6 at 73 kilometres. As I was leaving the CP I saw some fellas hollering ahead. They were having a cup of tea. Oh, my god. There is a tea stop. What a treat. I did not see it and only for these fellas were hollering, I probably would have passed it. That cup of sweet Moroccan tea at that point was as good as any pick me up.

I tucked in behind these lads. There were two South Africans, a Moroccan, a guy from France and one from what I think was Chile.

I would love to tell you I had the most amazing conversation of my life with these fellas. But I could not talk, so what I did was walk with them as part of their group. Without saying hello, introducing myself, partaking in any conversation. Nothing. I walked alongside these gentlemen for over 2 hours and they did not bat an eyelid as I eavesdropped on their conversations which ranged from south African tourism to Moroccan farming, Moroccan economics, sailing, sailing in south Africa, sailing in what I think was Chile, fitness, a story about abductions by al Shabab in Mali, how close we were to the Algerian border and its dangers and so on. It was an epic piece of conversation by these guys that I held onto like a crutch to help me burn another 10 kilometres. And believe me, at 15 minutes' pace a kilometre because of how slow dune hiking is, this crutch was so beneficial to my race performance that day.

And I didn't even thank them. Towards the end, I just walked off without even giving them the courtesy of a wave. It was probably one of the most selfish things I have even done in my whole life racing life. But it worked.

Arriving into CP 6 and an even quieter group of tents at 73 kilometres, I still needed another nap to get me further. But this time I set a timer on my watch for 20 minutes. I laid back and closed my eyes. Even though my timer was on. Even though there was an element of control to what I was doing, that voice popped up again.

"Barry, get the feck up."

I was like, I have a fucking timer on. What's your fecking problem? I looked at my watch. 10 minutes had elapsed. I listened to that voice. I got up and got going. 10 kilometres to 83 kilometres. Let's go get it done.

Starting off with 17 kilometres to go, I still needed to keep breaking down that distance. I would celebrate points along the way. The next point to be celebrated was to get to 80 kilometres. So all focus then shifts to getting to that milestone rather than the bigger picture. Once a kilometre beeped, I would say to myself "5.9 kilometres to go etc." and continually breaking down the distance to not overly stress the mind and body which were now at a complete state of fatigue.

It was so dark now. Some people could be found just lying back looking at the stars. I was mainly on my own and if I passed someone I would say hello but for the most part I would not get a reply. I was really alone, but I was not lonely. I was driving on to finish, fuelled for the most part with water, salt tablets and electrolytes. Considering I had no nutrition on board, outside of feeling tired, I was doing quite well.

I shone my light to the side and saw three sets of eyes with funny shaped ears looking directly at me from about 100 metres. If I were at home, I would say they were fox cubs but I have not a clue what they were. I kept walking, feeling I was being watched as I tried to reach those milestones.

80 kilometres came, 80 kilometres went. I celebrated. Internally I whooped and high fived myself. I tried to open a can of endorphins on myself. Break down 3.9 kilometres to the next CP, just breaking it down as I went. A blue glow came about. For a second, I thought for fuck's sake. I thought I would get back when it was dark. But swiftly told

myself to shut the feck up with your shite-talk and keep it real. You are where you are.

The final CP was weird. A weird sense of being stuck between the heavens. Stuck between the darkness and light. Having conquered so much, there were people sleeping. I took another nap even though I was just 7 kilometres from home. Setting my timer once more for 20 minutes. Closing my eyes, only to hear the sound of a now familiar voice.

"Barry, get the feck up."

I didn't argue this time, 10 minutes again. Buckled up and saddled up and I was out the gap. The blue glow increasing, which was great as the batteries in my head torch were dying and I could not be arsed changing the batteries. Taking the bag off my back, getting the new batteries, taking the old ones out and putting the new ones in was akin to bypassing the main frame.

At this stage, water would not really stay down so what I would do was rinse my mouth and spit it out. Just drinking the electrolytes bottle, rinsing and spitting as the light began to increase, I saw a familiar foe begin to pop its head up in the distance. How could it be that the sun is starting to come up again. It seemed to go so recently. I swear I could start to feel the heat once more and I really was not able for it. The sun looked like a super bright saucer, just poking itself up initially.

Everything is sore and fatigued, shoulders from the bag, hamstrings, joints. There is no more that can aid, only keep moving the feck forward.

A ridge comes into view and one believes nirvana is just behind that ridge line. Reach the ridge line and there is no nirvana. Once more, it happens until the finish line comes into view. We are met by media crew on the outskirts with still just over a kilometre to go. The sun rises a little further as the morning starts to become bright now. As I come into finish, what was one of the toughest experiences of my life, completing the long stage of 90 kilometres deep in the south Moroccan desert! I realised even then that something special happened to me over the latter part of those 22 and a half hours. Something in real time. Something subconscious, something supernatural, something that was a part of me but yet a higher power, something I may never explain where and why, but it happened, and it was amazing.

I cross the line and grab my tea. I receive congratulations only to retort as to how the administrators were doing. They were taken aback. And quite happy to be asked how they were doing on what was becoming another scorcher of a morning.

I grabbed my 6.5 litre allocation and made the final journey of that day to my tent.

I was the first man home. The Dutch guys were whooping "Hey Irrrissshhh" as they welcomed me back. First man into Tent 80 that week for the first time, it felt a job well done and I knew it would have helped my overall placing, however, not really knowing where the power came from.

Throwing the bottles to the side, I knew I had to get some body administration done. I checked a bite on my ankle, little bastard had caused my ankle to swell and I had red circular blotches everywhere so I took an anti-histamine and removed my gaiters and runners, although it took an age to remove the gaiters with the level of swelling. I was in agony. We are not supposed to take ibuprofen with the heat and dangers with cardiac arrest from dehydration, but I didn't give a feck and popped a pill. I rehydrated and thought about getting some protein in, but that was a bridge too far. I just lay there trying to elevate my legs.

My day was done, but the day was not over. Over the coming hours tent mates would arrive but I feared the worst for Alan having seen the condition he was in the previous day and I was worried for Aaron and Johnny, who were always shaving very close to the allotted time. People were coming back completely deranged. There was a 36-hour cut off. So if you were in early you got a rest day, but if at 36 hours no real rest day, just the evening to get your feet or what not sorted.

Everyone got back except Alan, who had to pull out with stomach problems. He had to wait another night with us until they transferred him back to Ouarzazate the following day.

Tent 80s 8 was now down to 7 but we were faring out well with what we were hearing about all the dropouts, bringing the total dropout rate to one of the highest recorded to date.

We were to get another 5-litre bottle of water that day, but more importantly, we were to get a bottle of coke.

If one has ever had a tough day running or racing in the heat, that can or bottle of coke, irrespective of how bad it is for you, is an amazing experience.

We received what I can describe as the old stubby bottle size of a Moroccan cola called Ice cola. After 4 days racing in the south Moroccan desert, I can tell you that the slightly cool bottle of syrupy cola was probably the most amazing culinary experience of my life. I brought the bottle back to my tent and on my own sipped it one sip at a time, savouring each mouthful like it was my last drink on death row. It was a truly amazing experience.

25. Thursday Day 5 The Marathon Stage 42.2km

---

3 Dropouts

I felt the last day to be quite sombre rather than buzzing as it was a hard day. Tent 80 Alan had to pull out on the long stage and was not racing the marathon stage having to be transferred to Ouarzazate. Our tent had done very well up to this point, whereas other tents were emptied or completely abandoned. Thankfully, I could eat dinner the night previously and I could also eat some porridge for breakfast. The word was the marathon stage was going to be even hotter again, which added to the general sense of trauma. Some lads in the tent were quite sick and Aaron was missing a significant amount of flesh off his forefeet at this stage, still managing to fist pump and say "Up the Deise" wherever possible. I worried for Johnny, he was literally on his hands and knees for 10 minutes getting sick to which Jack informed us that his previous night's dinner still looked like his previous night's dinner. On the last day, cruelty knew no limits as we began to get ourselves together and make our way to the final race line proper.

My intentions were the same as they were all week, run as much as possible until the heat made it too unbearable to do so. There were 650 odd metres of climbing to be done but no serious jebels. It was a very doable course if the heat was not in the 50's. I ran pretty well initially once through the sand dunes and early climbs. Passing the skull of a goat with some of its hair still visible, I found it quite apt and amusing to see but had no time for photo opportunities, as I just wanted to be finished. With the heat already starting to build greatly towards the first CP, we crossed our first tarmacadamed roads. Considering how long I spend running on roads, to stand on one if even only momentarily was a very funny feeling underneath my feet. It was so solid it made my legs feel wobbly. Like sea legs.

There were some family members including kids at the CP's. I thought this to be actually insane. I cannot imagine my wife and kids being there in that heat. It would have been so distracting as I would be then concerned about them. I tried my best to ignore these people that had chosen to be there on the final marathon stage. But it was quite strange, to see normal people with signs and flags or what not. Arriving at CP 2 I was doing running repairs with Sudocrem I was chafing quite badly on my left groin now. The chafing was quite long and wide and was raw. I had treated it the previous night and that morning, literally lumping the Sudocrem onto it but it needed to be topped up. Upon arriving at the tent in CP 2 I had a look again to see if I needed to reapply more Sudocrem only to find that all the stitching in the crotch of my run shorts which were tight like to knees had been obliterated. I was literally balls out.

Looking down at my 6-day-old sports specific shorts absolutely obliterated because of the extreme environmental conditions from heat, salt and sweat, they just literally fell apart at the seams, in no- way fixable, this material and its thread were simply dust. As dusty as the environment that they were tasked to operate in.

These were sport specific Raidlight running short tights specifically used for these events that lasted 6 days.

So great were these shorts that when my mother suggested bringing a spare pair, I dismissed her suggestion compared to all the knowledge I had about the requirements of this race, from fitness to equipment.

Thankfully I actually listened and brought about a spare pair and thus did not have the embarrassment of having a picture circulating of me finishing the toughest race of my life with my lad hanging out for the world to see.

Mothers, as always, know best.

I took off the Raidlights and put on the spare pair remembering, thank God, to also sun block the new skin areas that would be exposed with the shorter shorts.

Just before I was ready to leave two Scousers came into the tent. They were hilarious, informing some American that he looked like a model. We were all laughing and it was a welcome relief until the Yank started telling us all how he was urinating blood and the medical staff told him he was grand. Even a bit of banter ended with some story of something horrific coming out of an orifice.

I saddled up now with my new shorts and got going again, trying to get running again as I was feeling ok.

I think it was here between CP 2 and Cp 3 that we or maybe just me felt the greatest level of heat during the 37th edition of the Marathon Des Sables. Maybe I was so fatigued at this stage. I don't know. With some 18 odd kilometres left in my entire race week, I started to feel really wobbly. Normally, I would take 1.5 litres of water with me in two race bottles but this time I had another litre left inside my run bag. I needed every bit of it. I started to feel very woozy and lightheaded. I would try and run get a few hundred metres and then drop right back. I started to realise that pushing hard or even just pushing on could end up with dire consequences, so I really rowed back the pace and really focused on just finishing the day and race out. I really struggled in the dunes with its dead heat and faltered into CP 3.

One would think that everyone would be buzzing but it was a strange atmosphere, only to be broken up by the scouse comedy act that reckoned he saw the lights of a kettle on in the 4 x 4 as he accused the organisers of heating up the water with said kettle. The water was that hot to drink and also uncomfortable to drink. It nearly hurt drinking it. As I was still not able to eat any in race nutrition, the hot water seemed to slosh that bit more in my stomach.

It was here that I actually dumped all my in race nutrition as I could not eat any of it, anyway. I was delighted to be rid of all those sachets and packets of uneaten cliff block cubes. I had only ingested about half of the in race nutrition I had brought over and carried for the week.

The final leg of the day and race was just shy of 7km. It was stony and open, being able to see miles in the distance. Heads were down just to get this last stretch done. I could see a ridge line up ahead that people were getting animated at some sight, which I guessed to be the finish line. This gave a little motivation to at least try to run walk as much as possible. Crossing that ridge, we had two kilometres left and the finish line and bivouac was in full view. The last stretch still needed breaking down. I picked trees and ground types to break up the final two thousand metres.

The closer it got, the more animated the finish line seemed to get. One always runs the final few kilometres no matter what your condition or the race. I crossed in 7:30 hours.

Up ahead was Patrick Bauer himself. After being involved in the process for nearly 5 years and having seen the good, bad, and ugly of the organisation and organisations associated with the MDS I had wondered how I would react to him 1:1 in the flesh. I wondered would I fist bump or do a formal handshake. Would I show my views on his seemingly ruthless attitude with a shrug and make my point? Yet I had used mental imagery in the lead up to the race and during Patrick Bauer placing a medal around my neck.

I came face to face with him and he went "Irlandeees!"

"I am Patrick, I am Irlandeees." He asked me to give him a hug and much like many people have found over the last 37 years in the Marathon Des Sables for all his and his organisation's faults, he is a very charismatic man up close.

So I hugged the fecker. I got that medal around my neck and I walked away having completed the toughest foot race in the world. In one of its toughest editions owing to the heatwave that was experienced in Spain and Morocco over the period of that race.

I wasn't elated. I was not buzzing. I grabbed a cup of tea and we received the most beautiful bottle of Moroccan cola once more. I didn't even wait for a finisher photo. I just grabbed my water and made my way back to the tent to collapse one more time, where unfortunately, Johnny's kit was left as he had to pull out on stage one of the last day as sick as a dog. You really could not write it. Traumatic to the end.

As those that had survived the week filtered back, final numbers of DNF's started to be bandied about. The final figure seems to be about the 321 mark or 29.6% with apparently some French guy collapsing a few hundred metres from the line and not finishing the race.

It was over but it was not over as we still had the charity stage the following day, which was a 9km stage through the Merzouga dunes, the highest in Morocco. I finished that marathon in 289th place on the leader board out of 1085 starters and for someone who is never really happy with their own race result, I was genuinely happy with how I performed as I felt that anyone that managed to even get through a few days of racing that week was a warrior. Never mind those that finished it out.

The Tent 80 lads all made it home thereafter. Jack, Ian, Ronan, Seamus, and with 10 minutes to spare the Deise man, Aaron managed to get in just before the 12 hour cut off. Johnny had to spend the night with us after DNFing which was really hard on him and Alan was back in Ouarzazate.

I made my way to the Internet tent to send Alma a message. I had to put my sunglasses on inside because my first words were "I did it" as I bawled crying. Such was the release of stress and emotion of what had happened over the previous 6 days.

26. Friday 9km Charity Stage

The last and final stage of the Marathon Des Sables is the charity stage. This year, it was 9 kilometres which took in the highest dunes in Morocco, the Merzouga. To say we did not feel like doing it would be an understatement. It seemed cruel to expect those that were missing serious amounts of flesh from their feet to walk 9 kilometres in that heat. However, it was timed and compulsory and if you did not complete it, you could keep your medal but apparently you would not get a leader board standing.

Some run the final day, but most just walk it. Walk it with your tent. As we did. So Jack, Ian, Aaron, Ronan, Seamus and

I headed for the start line. Johnny was transferred via 4 x 4 at 6am that morning so at least he did not have to walk home medalless, which would have been extra cruel.

We were walking at the pace of the slowest man, which due to half a beer mat size loss of flesh from both feet – we flanked the Deise man, Aaron. All were emotional on the start line as this bubble we were living in for the last 9 days was coming to a close. The craic was getting going and Seamus landed a couple of really sharp jibes which were classic. We had one last address from Patrick and his shadow to which I can't even remember now was there another "Happy Birthday to you moment" as I was immune to the lyrics at that stage. "Highway to Hell" was belted out and we were off. Slowly walking in our kindergarten style yellow cotton t shirts, whilst not best to wear but at least they were clean.

We still needed all our water and this 9km stage even included a CP with extra water at which we all refilled our bottles for the final 3.7 kilometres through the dunes. Some peeled off from the caravan because of GI distress which just really showed how many competitors suffered right until the end.

People took sand from the dunes as a memento. For some reason I was not too bothered. I'm trying to stop hoarding things. As I write, I still have sand in my ears, anyway. I think grains will become part of my physical makeup going forward so I don't see the need.

I laughed when I saw the actual finish line. After skirting the highest dunes using whatever final bit of energy we had, there was a tiny incline to finish. It went from sand to concrete. Really signifying the last hold the sand had right up to the final few metres. I thought it was quite apt and symbolic. One had to be released from this race rather than win or conquer the course. The course had you until the last moment and it was decided when you could finish.

We spread out like a line of yellow taxis and what was left of Tent 80, 6 Irish lads finished in a line together up a slight concrete incline.

It was not a celebration, more an escape. After the traditional beautiful sugary cup of Moroccan tea, the elder statesmen of Tent 80 negotiated a price for a private transfer to Ouarzazate a 6-hour journey by bus that would be made easier with a people carrier.

A VW Caddy 7-seater was agreed on and a driver secured. We sat in begging for the A/C – I took the window seat, as I was still nauseous.

And that was that.

As with most of the race in the Marathon Des Sables, I never really looked behind myself. I only ever looked up or forward. I don't know why. It was like a subconscious decision. As that caddy pulled out driving forward, I felt relief.

Relief that the hardest thing I had signed up for both physically and mentally was now over. As a race I did not enjoy it, it was horrendous. Sometimes in races, be it Marathons, or day Ultras or Ironman's I would stick my head up and smile and go ‘this is awesome’ but in the 37th edition of the Marathon Des Sables at no point did I do this. It was that hard to complete, every moment was focused on the next moment and completion of whatever task lay ahead.

What was wonderful, however, was the bonds, teamwork and leadership that I was surrounded by. Tent 80 was a group of strangers. We had used technology such as Teams Meetings and WhatsApp groups to build a rapport and share information. But we went from technology to 8 men in a tent head to toe for comfort snap bang in the middle of a desert. We did not know each other, but yet we knew each other. We knew when someone was struggling; we knew how to have the piss taken out of them; we knew when to give space and we knew when someone needed an arm around the shoulder.

With the nature of groups, some are going to be under prepared and some are going to be over prepared. This created a very healthy balance of sharing. Things run out or items do not work out. Food was shared be that expedition foods dinners, in race nutrition, toilet paper, sudocrem, gurney goo, electrolytes, pins, batteries, the list goes on. One would not be stuck. I was over prepared yet one of my dinners was gone off and I had to get a dinner from Ian. We could support other's tents such as our Dutch friends in front who were running out of food. For the most part, we supported each other. Sharing pots of tea or meeting a man that was late in and carrying his water down for him. Listening to someone tell a story from home and just being open.

Each man was a success story in his own right. Yet each man was grounded and equal. When I am struggling, I just go quiet. This was picked up on quickly. Within 24 hours, lads were in tune with each other. I got a "You alright Barry" to which I replied "Ya 100%" even though my body was trying to figure out which end it was going to go into GI distress.

The 37th edition of the Marathon Des Sables, in my opinion, was a horrific race. A relentless attack from the elements with an extremely technical course which never seemed to let up be that underfoot and the sun beating down and everything in between. I will never do it again, I do not recommend that anyone do it after Ramadan, such as the time of the year.

That being said, even though the 37Th edition was horrendously horrific to complete, I and approximately 765 others completed it against all the odds. I think over time it will stand to every one of us in good stead. We all completed it for several reasons. All were extremely robust to do what was done. However, a small bit of luck was also needed to dodge everything from total GI distress, heatstroke, fevers, bites, and feet break down to name but a few afflictions.

It did not change me; it added something; it made me realise the power of my own higher self, which was called upon on the long stage. This had never happened before in such a positive manner to date as a 42-year-old and it was quite amazing to experience at the time and looking back now for the most part it is like unlocking a super power that seems to live on a subconscious level. This was the first time in my life that I actually felt or realised mental strength or one of its forms manifesting in my own higher voice driving me onwards.

For this I am grateful to the 37th edition of the Marathon Des Sables in unlocking this potential that I never knew existed. And having spent 8 nights on a desert floor, I realise how privileged I am to come home to my wife, kids, dog and a memory foam mattress.

I can feel a connection with the Sahara Desert in my heart, and I don't think it will ever leave. It is imprinted within me now. We all earned that.

27. Aftermath

Thankfully, with 15 years of experience in racing all types of races and distances, I understand my response to efforts be that hours, a day, or days. I understand the post-race blues when all the effort and energy that goes into something simply ends, then the mind searches either to be better or maybe go bigger. It may come across as being on the addiction spectrum, but I do not see it that way. I love the routine and the focus that these events give me and as much as I look forward to eating pizzas and the odd doughnut, after a few weeks a paunch returns and I start feeling a bit flabby and then I want to get back into some sort of athletic shape again.

Prior to Marathon Des Sables 2023, I had entered the Kerry Way Ultra 200kms trail race, but I knew even before I left for Morocco that I would not be doing it. I knew I was spent with all the efforts over the last number of years. I was done running each and every road in a 40 odd kilometre radius of Crossmolina and I just felt tired.

However, I was still quite surprised at how much was taken out of me with the Marathon Des Sables. Physically, I was fine with no obvious serious injuries, but internally I felt absolutely goosed. I would sleep from approximately 10pm to 8am the next morning for a number of weeks which is not like me as I like to rise before the kids get up when the house is quiet. My digestive system was still in bits for several weeks, having sporadic bouts of diarrhoea for no reason. That would go on and off over the course of 2 weeks after coming home. 4 weeks after I returned home, I got a chest infection. I have never been as bad for coughing and elected to go to Westdoc, an out of hours Doctors service, which is totally out of character for me! I was prescribed and took antibiotics for the first time in 20-odd years as the coughing was so bad.

This created a ‘stop start’ effect on returning to training. I was back for a week, then needed to take a week off to recover. I felt like I needed to go but my body was clearly telling me to hold off. Upon returning to full training, I found I was fine in the gym with resistance and quite enjoyed being coached again by my own Strength and Conditioning coach, Darren Siggins, doing an all over body work out with a little bit of an Olympic lifting component. But aerobically I found and still find running, mentally and physically tough to do.

Through my run coach Stephen Donnelly I am stepping back the distance and preparing for the Balllycastle half marathon in September 2023 with the idea of a sub 3-hour marathon effort or two in 2024, but it is really hard to get back into it psychologically. I would have expected this after 1 or 2 weeks but not 7 and 8 weeks out from race return.

Some may bounce back earlier, some may race long again this year, but I, for one, am happy that I am dropping back all intensities. I think the internal systems take an absolute hammering in these races from gut health, digestive, respiratory, cardiovascular and, obviously, mentally the levels of expansion of one's own mind can be life altering.

A few weeks after I came back from Morocco, I noticed that one of my toes was numb, yet again Googling when I should not have done so. The results showed everything from tight shoes to neural issues being potential causes. The feeling is slowly starting to come back into the toe, albeit not fully, so it should be grand, but it shows some of the knock-on effects of racing in such extreme races. Discussing this topic one morning in Crossmolina after the school run with yet another physio of mine, Liam Moffatt, we both discussed the strands of recovery and how the body reacts to play, be that on the grass or sand. One may feel that he or she is fine post marathon or ACL operation but is the mind on the same hymn sheet as that knee or toe as the body seems to have a way of finding out and exposing that weak spot, much like an engine management light with a fault in one's car.

I have not changed, but I am definitely a lot more confident having finished the race. Whereas previously I would not be sure of my abilities to do things, now there is no negative self-talk. Somehow, that desert has eradicated many of the things that I would have said to myself.

I feel like I have expanded my consciousness and closed some doors in my mind where negative self-talk and thoughts would roam the halls and recesses of my internal tributaries of conversation. The severity of what we all completed was so hard that one would have to dig out a new higher self to keep those feet moving in a forward direction. Previously sometimes I may have felt that I was about as useful as a chocolate teapot. I see this now as an old self, much like a reptile sheds its skin periodically, although I hope not to be viewed as reptilious, yet I have shed a skin. It is gone now, never to return–I have new brain skin and this skin does not cause me to talk to myself in such a negative way. In my opinion, placing myself in that race has allowed this to happen. I placed myself in an environment for a shed to take place.

I feel sorry for other competitors that now find themselves somewhat lost with this huge event completed and even sorrier for those who had to pull out of the race. It would gnaw away at one's soul for years. I dream about the Sahara now a lot. They say it is like the sea and with little on the horizon, one's mind has to expand. I dream about the dying light a lot in the evenings and made-up combinations of sunlight and trails for some reason that are more akin to a meditation than a run trail. It is quite trippy.

There is a draw with the Sahara. I could not understand those that had completed the race several times, continuing to return, some 17 or 18 times. But now I know why. It stays a part of you like nothing else I have experienced and draws you back in regularly with imagery, both real and imagined.

I swore I would never return to that place, yet I will not be offloading any kit. I swore I would only return to Morocco to surf, yet I only dream of shale trails and not the right-hand points of Taghazout.

Recently I heard the American Ultra Endurance athlete, podcaster and all-round cool guy, Rich Roll, say that "we overestimate what we can do in a year and we underestimate what we can do in 10 years".

I look to the next 10 years, becoming a beginner again, starting from the ground up with something different but yet same, a challenge that I wonder if it is something I really want to do or something to fuel my ego. Maybe over the coming months I will seek out and start to figure out what is driving this in the first place before I become obsessed. Sowing seeds, manifesting, learning the basics, becoming an uphill athlete, being physically, mentally and spiritually ready to go should the opportunity arise. I will never be the greatest of all time, but I was born in January thus a Capricorn, thus a GOAT, the type of 4-legged creature that finds itself on top of mountains much like I may be within 10 years, on top of Everest.

Time will tell.

About the Book

"Baby Dara And The Sahara" details the ups and downs over a 5 year period of life for Mayo man, Barry Loftus, and his family. It commences with a very problematic pregnancy, moving on to the ups and downs of a Covid cancelled race which dragged on for 3 years after it should have been completed.

It tells the story of a Dad and some of his experiences in dealing with his wife's pregnancy, how he manages to keep his business ticking and a family home with two other "smallies", be present for his wife and continue to live as healthy a life as possible.